WHICH WAY FREEDOM?

JOYCE HANSEN

AN AVON CAMELOT BOOK

AVON BOOKS, INC.
1350 Avenue of the Americas
New York, New York 10019

Copyright © 1986 by Joyce Hansen Nelson
Published by arrangement with Walker and Company
Visit our website at **http://www.AvonBooks.com**
Library of Congress Catalog Card Number: 85-29547
ISBN: 0-380-71408-6
RL: 4.8

First Avon Camelot Printing: February 1992

CAMELOT TRADEMARK REG. U.S. PAT. OFF. AND IN OTHER COUNTRIES, MARCA REGISTRADA, HECHO EN U.S.A.

Printed in the U.S.A.

OPM 20 19

Author's Note

All of the characters in *Which Way Freedom?* are fictional. However, the massacre at Fort Pillow, Tennessee, was an actual event. Detailed interviews of Union soldiers who survived the slaughter at the fort can be read in the Fort Pillow Massacre Report #65, Joint Committee on the Conduct of the War, April 20, 1864.

The First South Carolina Volunteers was one of the original black regiments to be mustered into the Union Army. Colonel T. W. Higginson, commander of the regiment, said: "The fate of the Confederacy was decided by Sherman's march to the sea. . . . Next to the merit of those who made the march was that of those who held open the door. That service will always remain among the laurels of the black regiments."

Black soldiers were involved in the intense fighting in Tennessee, Mississippi, and Virginia. The Twenty-fifth Corps was the first army corps composed entirely of black regiments, of which there were thirty-two. Some 200,000 blacks fought in the Civil War.

I hope this book gives the reader a deeper understanding of African American participation in that period of American history.

One

Question: *Have you been a slave?*
Answer: *Yes, sir.*
Question: *How long have you been in the army?*
Answer: *About two months.*

Report #65-United States Congress
Joint Committee on the Conduct of the War
April 20, 1864

April 12, 1864
At one time he'd simply been Obi, the slave of John Jennings. When he joined the army he was told he had to have a family name, so he used his former master's last name. His superior officers addressed him as Private Jennings, but he wouldn't allow his fellow soldiers to call him that—just Obi.

He dreaded the sound of his name at roll call. It was as ill-fitting as his clumsy boots.

"Private Jennings!" the sergeant yelled.

"Here, suh!" he yelled back, standing at attention and holding his rifle against his thigh. He kept his head erect while his large, deep-set eyes stared directly ahead, as the Yankee drillmasters had taught him. His tall frame was as lean and straight as a young pine.

The sergeant continued talking after he took the roll call. Like most of the men of the Sixth U.S. Heavy Artillery of Colored Troops, Sergeant Johnson was an ex-slave.

"You men be alert. General Forrest an' his Rebs burn

1

down Union City an' kill everything movin'," he said, rocking his stocky body back and forth in time to his words. "Union City ain't far from here." The sergeant's eyes, as round as the gold-colored buttons on his blue jacket, scanned the black and brown faces of his men. Some of them were as old as forty-five, but most were younger—many as young as seventeen or eighteen.

All of the soldiers wore soft forage caps, which a few of the younger men, including Obi, had turned a little to the sides of their heads.

Obi was nineteen or twenty. He didn't know his exact age, but he remembered that he was about ten years old when he became the property of the Jennings family. Even now, he'd still get a slight throbbing in his temple when he recalled his mother's screams as he was taken from her.

"Severe punishment to any man sleepin' or even lookin' in the wrong direction when you on duty. This a war, not a rabbit hunt. You boys smell somethin' funny, start shootin'."

"Better hope it ain't him we smell," the soldier behind Obi mumbled. His name was Joseph Chaney, and he had joined the army at the same time Obi had.

Obi's smooth, black face creased into a slight smile at the man's joke. The soldiers of Company B had nicknamed Sergeant Johnson "the Driver," saying that he was like those slaves on the plantation whose job it was to make sure the other slaves did their work.

"Save the Union!" Johnson said as he finished, holding up his fist. Some of the men moaned, some laughed at his customary dismissal. Obi ran out of the fort with the other troops who had guard duty. Private Thomas West caught up to him, and they walked down the slope of the steep hillside to their guard post. This was the river side of the hill. The Mississippi River was hidden below them by the predawn darkness and by the trees, bushes, and fallen timber along the side of the hill.

"The Driver is trying to scare us into being soldiers," Thomas said. "The only things we've been fighting since we've been here is river rats."

Obi adjusted his rifle so that it fit comfortably on his arm. "Some of them rats may be havin' grey coats yet," he said dryly.

As they continued walking down the bluff, they crossed a level portion of ground situated below the fort. Here were the shacks and log huts where the white soldiers of the Thirteenth Tennessee Battalion were quartered. The black troops were quartered up the hill inside the fort in tents.

The weary voices of men coming off night guard duty reached them as they continued their walk down the hill. The croaks and clicks of frogs and insects blended with the voices of the soldiers.

When they reached the bottom of the hill, they turned left and walked toward their post. Their job was to watch several buildings near the riverbank where supplies of food, arms, ammunition, clothing, and medicines were stored.

A blacksmith's shop and a general store stood a few yards behind the building. Log cabins and broken-down shacks were sprawled near the stores. The soldiers called this cluster of homes and shops "the town."

Instead of going directly to their post, they continued to the river's edge. Side by side, leaning against a tree, they faced the river in front of them.

"I don't think the Rebels are coming here," Thomas said. "The Driver is just making himself feel important, Obi. That's why he keeps telling us the enemy is just around the bend."

Obi still hadn't gotten used to seeing Thomas's rich, brown face and hearing the nasal Yankee accent coming out of his full African mouth. Thomas, with his large head and wide, dark eyes, was born in the North and was the first black that Obi had met who had not been a slave at some point in his life. About the same age as Obi, he had become a brother and a friend in spite of his Yankee accent.

"Why you think they not go try an' take this fort back?" Obi asked.

Thomas turned away from the river and gazed in the direction of the fort. "If they charge that hill, we can swat 'em down like flies," he said, moving his hand swiftly back and forth. Thomas was shorter than Obi, and he had quick, nervous movements.

"Them was some awful stories we hear about what happen in that Union City," Obi said. "And Major Booth been lookin' terrible worried lately."

"Stories grow with the telling." Thomas faced the river again. "He's just listening to the same old tales we hear about how cruel General Forrest is."

Thomas don't know these Rebs—they comin' back for their fort, Obi said to himself.

Two young black boys came toward them from the direction of the log cabins. The boys lived with their parents and another brother and sister in the last cabin closest to the woods. They stopped in front of Obi and Thomas and grinned as they saluted. "Right face!" they shouted together.

Obi and Thomas returned their salute. "Good morning, little generals," Thomas laughed. The children ran up the hill to the officers' quarters, where they worked as servants. The whole family had run away from a Mississippi plantation when the war started, and the father was one of the cooks at the fort. "This war the best thing happen to me. First time in my life I earn a wage," he'd told Obi.

Obi picked up his rifle. "Now we can go," he said.

"Yes," Thomas said, nodding. "Can't leave until we salute the generals." He chuckled. For the past month, greeting the boys had become a part of Obi and Thomas's morning ritual. They turned away from the river and walked back toward their post, but instead of stopping at the buildings, Obi kept walking toward the woods that lay behind the cabins and shacks.

"Where are you going?" Thomas asked, walking quickly to catch up to Obi's long strides. They passed the general store and the log cabin from which the young boys had just come.

"Want to check on somethin'," Obi said. Aside from the two children, no one else had stirred yet. Only Obi and Thomas walked along the dusty, streetless town.

Obi stopped walking as they entered the woods. "You can't see your hand before your face," Thomas complained. "We don't have to patrol these woods. Our pickets are already out there. What're you looking for, anyway?"

"A sign. Can't see nothin', though. Don't know who hidin' here."

Thomas shifted his weight from one foot to the other. "You don't believe in magic, do you?"

"You can figure words and letters, Thomas, but you don't read other signs." Thomas had been teaching Obi how to read, and Obi marvelled at how Thomas could understand what a squiggly line meant. It seemed strange to him that his friend could read but couldn't figure out obvious things.

"I want to see if someone been in here. Maybe they diggin' or clearin' path—changin' the woods," Obi said. "I readin' the woods."

"Changing the woods? Woods are always changing and everything looks the same all at once."

"That's why you got lost in here," Obi said. He turned around and they strolled back to their post.

"I wasn't lost that time. Just a little confused is all." Thomas smiled good-naturedly.

Obi rarely smiled, but when he did it was a surprise to see how straight and white his teeth were and how handsome his long face actually was. He grinned now. "You lucky I find you before the Driver. I know woods. Been in woods all my life."

"I've been in New York all of mine and wish I was there now. Well, Obi, did you smell something funny, like the Driver said?"

"No," Obi laughed. "I go back when it lighter."

They passed the cabins again, and Obi pointed toward the fort and the ravine above it. "That's what needs checkin'—that ravine."

Thomas sighed. "The pickets are out there. We'll hear firing soon enough if any Rebels show." He stopped walking and shook his large head. "They're not coming back, Obi. They have better things to do."

Obi realized that Thomas was trying to convince himself. He knew as well as Obi that the fort was important because of the river. When they reached their post, the two young men sat beside each other on the steps of one of the buildings and waited for the town to wake. As the calls of the birds became louder, Obi saw the elder sister of the two "generals" come out of her cabin, holding her baby brother's hand. She carried a pail and was headed toward the well behind her house.

Thomas saw her too and leaned forward with his elbows on his knees. His wide eyes seemed to get wider. "That's a pretty girl, Obi. I'm going to sit here for ten minutes and think about her."

Obi wanted to reflect also. Each time he saw the girl in her long, homespun dress with her little brother, he thought about Easter and Jason. He thought about the journey that had taken him from slavery and the Jennings farm in South Carolina. So much had happened to bring him to Fort Pillow, Tennessee, on the Mississippi River.

Two

Slavery days was hell . . . I could tell you about it all day,
but even den you couldn't guess de awfulness of it.

Delia Garlic, ex-slave
From *Voices from Slavery*

July 1861

Obi rose from his crouching position. The mule stood next
to him, swishing its tail. The two sacks tied behind the
animal were filled with tobacco leaves. Guessing by the
position of the sun, Obi figured it was about three o'clock.
They'd already been working for eight hours. He caught a
glimpse of Easter in the next field. All he actually saw was
part of her homespun dress, which looked like a dab of
white paint on a sea of green leaves. Little Jason was stumbling over to her, carrying a bucket of water.

Master John Jennings and his wife, Martha, were hidden
by the tall stalks of tobacco. They were in a field that was
in front of the field where Obi worked. He turned around,
looking in the direction of the farmhouse and the barn.
Wilson, Master John's brother, was by the barn bundling
tobacco leaves. His black slouch hat hid his face. Two
brown-and-white hounds lay in the shade of a magnolia
tree nearby.

Hope Wilson keep he evil self there, Obi said to himself.

7

Pushing back his wide straw hat, he wiped his forehead and watched Jason walk toward Master John and Martha with the water.

Obi, Easter, and Jason were slaves. They worked on the Jennings farm in South Carolina, nearly thirty miles from Charleston. Easter was about thirteen and Obi, sixteen or seventeen. Jason was seven years old and the only one who knew his correct age because he was born on the farm.

The children were the only slaves the Jennings owned and were their most valuable property—worth more than the mules and the mare. Wilson was part owner of the farm too, but up until recently, he'd hardly ever been around. He'd left years ago and came back only for rare visits.

John Jennings would tell people that his brother was a soldier of fortune. "Makin' money through adventuresome activity," he would say. Wilson had worked on merchant ships and sometimes on slavers. It was Wilson who had brought Obi, Easter, and Jason's mother, now dead, to the farm. He came home permanently when the Civil War began.

The children fared better than many other slaves. They ate the same rice, grits, beef, pork, vegetables, and salt fish the family did. They weren't beaten and were given warm clothes in the winter. The Jennings had no children of their own. John, a lanky, quiet man, wasn't comfortable in the role of master the way his brother was. He refused to "rule by the lash," and he once told Wilson as much.

Lately, however, though he hated to admit it to his brother, John Jennings recognized that having two healthy, young slaves like Easter and Obi was a sound investment. Even Jason might be worth some money one day.

Martha did not approve of the idea of owning other people, but she had to keep her feelings to herself. Every time she saw a group of slaves chained together, being shipped from the Charleston slave market to some other part of the state, she'd say to herself, *We're goin' to pay for this sin one day.*

Still, Obi had often thought of running away to find his mother. Time had blurred the image of her face from his mind, but he'd never forgotten her name—or the sounds of her screams when he was sold away. He also remembered being in a dark place and a man who held his hand. Most of all, he remembered how much he had missed her. Sometimes he heard her cries when birds screeched or the wind howled during a storm.

Obi's mother had been a slave on a large rice plantation on one of the Sea islands off the South Carolina coast. Obi dreamed of returning to the island, finding her, and escaping with her to Mexico, though he hadn't the faintest idea of where Mexico might be. It was merely the name of a place he'd heard that slaves ran to.

Making plans for running was a secret game that Obi played with his friend Buka. Buka was an old African who lived by the creek where the farm ended. The children of his last master didn't want him—said he was too old and difficult. "I so old, no one want to buy or sell my hide," he'd tell Obi.

For Obi, Buka was a living adventure who loved to talk and tell stories. Most of the tales were about running away and about his memories of Africa. "We was growin' rice in Africa too. That's why these Carolina slavers like to steal us coastal Africans," he'd say.

The most important story Buka told was Obi's family history, as Buka called it.

"Your mother tall with skin like a beautiful dark night. She eyes sit deep inside she face like yours. She cry fierce when the man take you from her to put you on the boat.

"Since I being sold with you an' the others, I tell her that I take care of you. I put my arms around you because you yellin' to wake the dead too. As we walk on the boat, the last thing she cry to you is, 'Remember your mama's name. Your mama name Lorena.' You still cling to me when we reach the slave pen at the Charleston market. You was six or seven years old.

"Then that ship captain buy you an' take you to his house in Charleston. Master Graves buy me an' bring me to this area.

"The last thing I say to you when we separate is 'Remember your mama name.' When Wilson bring you to the farm three years later, I know it you because you have your mama face, an' I never forget she face.

"I say to you, 'What your mama's name?' You say, 'Lorena.' "

Obi remembered the rest of the story himself. He remembered cleaning and working on the captain's ship when it was in port and the black cook in the captain's house who beat Obi every time the captain's wife beat her—which was often.

He remembered the day Wilson and the captain argued over money. The captain pointed to Obi and said, "Take the nigger in payment, and that's more than you deserve."

"Here the water, Obi," Jason said, interrupting his thoughts. Obi dipped the tin cup and drank the cold, sweet water down quickly. He dipped the cup again.

Jason wiped his small face with his shirttail. His thin, bare feet were almost indistinguishable from the soil.

"When you take the tobacco to Master Phillips, I come too?"

"It ain't up to me no more."

There was nothing Jason liked better than going to the Phillips plantation, where there were children his age. The plantation was a mile west of the farm. Many of the small farmers in the county sold their crops to the Phillips plantation, with its large number of acres and slaves. John Jennings had his tobacco cured and separated according to quality at the plantation before selling it at the market.

"I ask Mistress," Jason said. "She let me go."

"She can't say if you go neither. You ask Wilson or Master John."

"I 'fraid of Wilson."

Obi drank more water. "Stay out he way."

Jason kicked the dirt.

"You ain't no more baby," Obi said. "You finish shellin' the peas?"

"No," Jason mumbled.

Obi grabbed Jason's ear and the boy cried out. "Is *that* I mean!" said Obi. "You ain't finish your task an' you askin' to go to plantation. You know Wilson gonna take that up with you. I keep tellin' you, do your task so he don't bother you!"

Jason picked up the bucket. "Mistress won't let him beat me," he whined.

Obi bent down and started pulling the bottom leaves from the stalk of a plant. "What she do? Wilson catch you when she ain't lookin'."

Obi knew that Jason was probably right. As long as John and Martha were there, Wilson wouldn't beat them—but he wanted Jason to learn how to protect himself. "Stop lettin' Wilson catch you with your britches down, Jason."

"Ain't got no britches." Jason's eyes were teary. His long shirt was made of sacking and stopped at his skinny knees. Obi stifled a laugh.

"Finish shellin' an' go help Easter. I ask Wilson or Master if you can come with me if I go tomorrow mornin'."

Jason's little face lit up. "You think they be more soldiers there?"

"I don't know. Get on to your task now."

"Thank you, Obi," Jason sang out as he ran, swinging the bucket and tripping over his own feet.

Last month, when Obi and Jason were at the plantation, they saw Tyler, the eldest Phillips son, ride off to join the Confederate Army. Obi remembered how handsome Tyler had looked sitting on his horse with a finely crafted saber gleaming at his side. "Be back for supper—this won't take long," he had said cheerfully as he waved to the house servants. They had gathered in the yard to see their young master off.

Jeremiah, one of the Phillips's slaves, had ridden off with

him. The saber and Jeremiah were gifts to Tyler from his father. That night Obi had gone to Buka's shack. "You think this war be good or bad for us?" he had asked him.

"I don't know," Buka had said. "We have to watch an' wait. North an' South fight, but these white men still be brothers."

Obi worked faster now, even though the sun felt as if it were burning a hole in his back. If he could get a good portion of his field done, he'd be able to help Easter so she'd have a sizeable crop picked before sundown.

An hour later, he looked over at the girl. She didn't seem to be making much progress. His heart sank when he turned and saw Wilson walking toward the fields, pulling his wide, black slouch hat over his eyes. He was of medium height but thick and muscular.

Peace gone now, Obi said to himself and sighed.

"This all you git done?" Wilson said loudly as he approached Obi. "We ain't goin' to be doin' this come next month."

"It be done 'fore then," Obi said quietly as he continued working.

"I know it'll be done. I'm makin' sure of that." His face was red and coarse from his days on the sea, and now the Carolina sun.

"And what's wrong with that gal?" He stared in Easter's direction. "She sick or somethin'?" The veins in Wilson's temple throbbed.

Obi knew that an answer wasn't expected of him. *Workin' best she can. Just a girl. Ain't no mule,* he thought.

Wilson strode as if he were balancing himself on a ship's deck, heading toward the field where Easter worked. Obi took his mule back to the barn so he could empty the sacks now filled with tobacco leaves. He piled the leaves on top of the others that had to be bundled. A little later he trudged back to the fields. Instead of going to his field, however, he walked hesitantly over to Wilson and Easter. Easter looked helpless as Wilson pointed to the leaves.

"Gal, I'll wrap my belt 'round your legs and have you runnin' through these leaves like a jack rabbit if you don't stop playin'," he yelled at her.

Her full bottom lip trembled as she stared at the ground. Obi wanted to fling Wilson to the other end of the field.

"What do you want?" Wilson shouted when he saw Obi watching them.

"I help her, suh," Obi said.

"You got your own work!" The veins in his temple looked as if they might burst.

"I do mine an' help her. The crop be in 'fore month end, sure."

Wilson stuck his stubby finger in Obi's face. "This is July twenty-fifth. You've got six days. I don't care what my brother says. That crop ain't in, your hide goin' to be tanned good. Hers too." He stared from one to the other. "Remember this. War or no war, they're still buyin' and sellin' black tails in the Charleston market. Git rid of y'all and buy me some real hands."

He walked away from them. Easter's small shoulders slumped. She was short and slender, and her thick braids were covered with a piece of blue cloth to protect her head from the sun. "He mean as a snake," she said, near tears. Her hands were black and gummy like Obi's from the tobacco leaves. A smudge streaked across one of her brown cheeks. Her lively eyes often curled easily into a smile when she laughed, but now they looked tired and frightened.

"He ain't sellin' or beatin' nobody. I never let him beat you. Master John wouldn't let him either. Just evil 'cause he have to work like us," Obi said.

"Obi, you touch him, he try an' kill you."

"No he won't. Give me a lash or two," he said, smiling. "Then Master John stop him."

"I don't like talk of sellin'," she said, frowning. "We always been together. You, me, an' Jason." She yanked a leaf off the stalk. "An' why he so set about the crop bein' in 'fore August?"

"I been wonderin' the same thing," Obi answered. He brushed the back of his hand lightly over the two lines that appeared on her forehead whenever she was worried. "Stop botherin' you self. Wilson just like a barkin' dog. Ain't gonna bite," he said bravely.

Easter flexed her tired fingers. "Master John never drive us to finish croppin' 'fore August."

Jason, struggling across the field with another bucket of water, headed for John and Martha. When he finished with them, he brought Easter and Obi their water.

"You finish that shellin'?" Obi asked him.

He nodded. "I help you an' Easter now."

Easter smiled at Jason. "Sing us a song. Make time go fast."

Jason sang a song he'd learned from the children on the Phillips plantation as he pulled the leaves from a stalk. His voice was high-pitched and clear. Easter picked up the tune and soon had the words. Obi never sang, but a peacefulness came over him as he listened to their young voices.

They worked continuously for the next two hours until Obi stopped. "Go get us some water," he called to Jason, motioning to Easter to come and sit beside him. They watched Jason run to the well in the yard close to the house. Wilson came out of the barn and called Jason to him.

"Get no water now," Obi muttered in disgust. Jason was walking over to Wilson when Jessie, the overseer from the Phillips plantation, rode into the yard.

"Wonder what happen?" Easter asked.

Obi and Easter watched in silence as Jessie climbed off his horse and tied it to a tree. He and Wilson spoke for a minute, then they both walked quickly to the field where John and Martha were still working.

Jason raced toward Obi and Easter. "Tyler dead!" he yelled from the hedges where the field began. "Overseer say Yankees kilt him!"

Three

If there is no struggle there is no progress.

Frederick Douglass, abolitionist, ex-slave
From a speech given at Canandaigua, New York
August 4, 1857

When Jason reached them, Easter bent down and peered closely into his eyes. "What else you hear them say?"

"Nothin'. Just what I tell you. What's a Yankee?" His brown eyes were wide with wonder.

Easter straightened up, adjusting her head wrap. "Ain't quite sure, but I think a person from the North. I find out tonight from Mistress." Since Easter and Jason slept in the house, she knew everything that happened or was about to happen. Obi slept in the hayloft in the barn.

Obi turned to Jason. "Get that water 'fore Wilson find somethin' else for you to do." He and Easter sat on the ground waiting for Jason to come back.

"I wonder if Buka know about Tyler?" Obi said.

"People been sneakin' in an' out the shack all day bringin' the news. You know he know."

When the red sun slid behind the oak grove, Martha Jennings called Easter to help her prepare supper. "I take the mules back," Obi told her. "You go on to Mistress."

Obi led the mules to the barn while Jason went to bring

in the cows from the pasture that spread out behind the house. As Obi neared the barn, John Jennings came in behind him. He left his mule so that Obi could empty his and Martha's sacks and finish bundling the leaves.

Obi welcomed the smell of hay and animals in the cool darkness of the barn. Over the years this had become his own private place. He put the mules in their stalls. Jason brought in the cows and then clambered up the ladder and threw down hay for the mules. "When you think we goin' to Master Phillips?" he called down to Obi.

"Don't know." Obi hoped Jason wouldn't bother him with a lot of questions.

"Guess Master Phillips get them Yankees for killin' Tyler . . ."

"Guess so," Obi said as he placed a bundle of leaves under the work table. "When you done feedin' the mules, make sure all the pigs in the pen an' the chickens inside their coop."

"Obi, what you think the—"

"Quit all that talkin' an' tend to your work," Obi said.

Jason finished feeding the animals in silence and ran out of the barn. Obi hadn't meant to be nasty to Jason, but he wanted to think about Tyler's death and the war. He understood none of it except that Yankees were killing the people who held him in bondage. Maybe this was a good time to try to get to the island.

A half hour later, Jason walked slowly back into the barn. "All the pigs an' chickens in," he said.

"Put up the harnesses an' straighten them tools. Then we wash."

Jason quietly did as he was told, standing on the milking stool Obi had made for him so that he could hang the harnesses on their hooks. He stepped off the stool and rested the pitchforks against the wall near the spare ax handles.

"If we carry the leaves to plantation tomorrow mornin', I ask Master can you come," Obi said.

Jason grinned and almost tripped over the milking stool.

"Don't run your mouth. Easter tell us what she find out 'bout Tyler when we eat."

After they finished their chores, they went to the shed behind the barn and washed themselves in the tin tub. When they were done, they carried the tub to the creek near the oak grove to fill again so they'd have water for the following day.

When the tub was full, Obi hesitated. He couldn't see it in the darkness, but Buka's shack was only a few feet away.

He said to Jason, "I goin' to see Buka. Keep watch for me. You see Wilson or Master, then sing that song you was singin' today an' I come back."

Obi didn't expect that anyone would come looking for him—the family should be eating by now—but as Obi and Jason lifted the tub out of the creek, they were both startled by the sound of someone stepping on twigs and dried leaves. Master John walked over to them. "I was lookin' for you. Carry that water back and then clean me and Master Wilson's boots."

"Yes, suh," Obi said.

Jennings started to walk away and then turned around. "Don't none of you leave this farm 'less I write you a pass. And you stay away from that old man, Obi."

Obi almost asked him, "Which old man?" hardly believing that he was talking about Buka. He could understand why Jennings wouldn't want him to be with Buka if there was work to do, but otherwise he had never stopped Obi from going. Sometimes on Sundays he would even let Obi fish with Buka all day. Master John turned and stomped off quickly. The twigs and branches crunched noisily under his feet.

"Why he angry?" Jason whispered loudly as they lifted the tub again.

"Hush." Obi wondered the same thing. Master John wasn't

a jovial man, but Obi had never known him to be angry for no reason. They carried the tub back to the shed, sloshing water as they went along.

When they returned to the barn, two pairs of boots had been placed near the barn door.

"Why Master don't want you to see Buka?" Jason asked.

"Don't know." Obi pulled the milking stool from under the hayloft and picked up one of the worn black boots. "Bring my cleanin' rags an' stop askin' me questions I can't answer!"

Obi was glad when Easter finally called them to eat. Maybe she found out something that would explain Master John's new rules.

Jason and Obi carried the cleaned and polished boots to the house and left them outside each man's bedroom door. Martha and the two men were in the sitting room. The smell of savory stew came from the large kitchen where Easter tended to the cooking. Lately, Easter did more cooking than Martha. During the winter months, she and Obi were hired out to the Phillips plantation, where Easter worked with the cooks. As she grew more experienced, Martha depended on her to do a lot of the cooking and baking on the farm. Obi worked with the Phillips's carpenter. The money they earned helped the Jennings family live through the winter.

The adults had finished eating their dinner, and now the children ate what was left over. Easter spooned stew onto each wooden plate. Obi took three battered tin cups from the fireplace and filled them with milk. Jason sat quietly at the oak table. They could hear Wilson's and John's voices in the sitting room but couldn't tell what they were saying.

Obi scooped a spoonful of the thick stew as Easter sat across from him and Jason. Easter bowed her head and reached for their hands, but Obi pulled his away and started eating. Easter's voice was soft as a feather as she said the grace. Jason lowered his head, but his eyes were wide open, staring hungrily at the food.

When Easter finished she said, "Obi, Mistress say we have to thank God for this food."

"What I have to be thankful for?" He took another spoonful of stew.

"Least we eat the same food Master an' Mistress do. Master Phillips give his people a peck of corn an' some salt pork for the whole week."

"I should get more than this, hard as I work today." He took a long drink of milk. "Now tell me what you hear about Tyler."

She leaned closer to Obi. "Mistress tell me the whole story,'" she whispered. "Was a big battle in a place called Virginny. They bring he back in a box this mornin'. Mistress say nobody know whether it really Tyler in there. Say they put a body in a box an' send it home to Master Phillips because Tyler was a officer."

Jason listened so intently that he stopped eating. "Why they kilt Master Tyler? He bad?"

"Hush," Easter and Obi said to Jason at the same time. Obi recalled how proud and handsome Tyler had looked sitting on his horse.

Easter took a bite of stew and continued her story. "Mistress say most of them what die they bury right where they fall."

"What happen to Jeremiah?" Obi asked.

"Mistress ain't say. Guess one of them cannonball get him too. Mistress seem spooked—like somethin' scarin' her."

"Maybe Master John scare of somethin' too," Obi said and told her that they were ordered not to leave the farm without a pass.

Easter rested her spoon on the plate. "Somethin's terrible wrong. Master evil as a buzzard when he come inside. Say somethin' to Mistress about the war startin' for real. An' Yankees—just a hollerin' about Yankees. Act like Wilson. He quiet when I walk in. Won't say nothin' in front of me."

Jason picked up his cup and drank down the milk. "Maybe they scare Yankee get them too," he said quietly.

"Hush, boy," Easter said. "What you know about such things?"

They finished their meal in silence, listening to the muf-fled voices of the men. After they cleaned the kitchen, Obi went back to the barn. He decided not to try to see Buka that night but to wait until the next day.

Obi was sorry Tyler had to die, but he was glad for his funeral. He, Easter, and Jason would be alone while the Jennings went to the plantation. He'd been in the field since sunrise and was relieved when, at ten o'clock, he saw John Jennings mount his horse. Martha and Wilson climbed into the wagon. Both men wore black frock coats. Martha wore her black bonnet and dress. Wilson had on the slouch hat he always wore.

After the adults left, Easter and Jason walked out to the field where Obi worked. Jason carried some water.

"Wilson make a fuss this mornin'," Easter said. "Say we poor farmers. No need for him to go to the funeral. Too much work to do."

Obi dipped his cup in the bucket. "He want to stay here to bother us."

Easter squinted her eyes in the sun's glare. "Wilson say Mistress should go an' he an' Master stay an' work. Master say if they don't go an' show they sorry Tyler dead, Master Phillips never buy a pea or a ear of corn from them again."

"I wish they stay the whole day," Obi said. He called to Jason, who had taken the mule and started working the rows of tobacco. Easter's eyes curled up at the corners as she smiled. "Jason actin' like a little man today," she said.

"I goin' to see Buka. You stay by the creek. Anyone come, start singin'," Obi said as Jason ran to him.

Easter frowned. "You shouldn't, Obi. You know what Master say last night. Suppose you not here when they come back?"

Obi pulled his straw hat over his eyes. "They not comin' back for a while. I not stayin' long."

Buka's shack looked like a box with a smokestack on top. Inside, the only furniture he had was a small, rough table. The pallet he slept on was near the wall.

The old man sat cross-legged in front of the fireplace, a cup of meal coffee in his hand. Buka used to hunt and fish and grow a few vegetables. During the cropping season, the Phillips plantation, and even some of the smaller planters, had used him as a field hand. He would do the work in exchange for food and clothing.

For the past year, however, Obi noticed that a change had come over Buka. He seemed to shrivel up like a prune, his shoulders becoming round and his eyes red and weak looking. He didn't fish or hunt anymore and rarely walked farther than the creek.

Buka knew almost everyone in the county. When Charles Graves, his most recent master, had died, Buka was the eldest slave in the estate. He'd told Obi that story also.

"When they put me on the auction block, I make myself look sick an' older than I already was. Slump my shoulder like so."

He'd hunch his shoulders and Obi would laugh. "Then I had my head like so, like my eyelid can't raise." He'd turn his head to one side and barely open his eyes.

"Then I curl all my finger like I have the rheumatism bad. No one buy me. An' that's the story of how old Buka free to this day."

Buka was old then but still strong enough to go from farm to farm, doing odd jobs in the county. He'd even worked for John Jennings during tobacco-cropping season.

Obi loved that time, with Buka telling stories while they picked tobacco leaves. Back then, there was no Wilson around to bother them.

Now that Buka was very old and weak, slaves from the neighboring farms and plantations visited him, bringing him food and news.

To the whites, he was merely an old slave who'd outlived his usefulness. To the blacks, he was an African elder, deserving respect for having lived so long and survived so much.

Obi sat in front of Buka and handed him a piece of corn bread he'd saved from breakfast. Buka looked away from the fireplace.

"What's troublin' you?" Buka asked. He offered Obi a cup of meal coffee. Obi disliked the bland liquid because he knew the taste of real coffee, but he took the cup so that Buka wouldn't be offended.

"You know Tyler dead?"

"I know. The funeral today. Three people come yesterday to tell me."

"What you think about this war? You think it time for me to go to the island, look for my ma?"

Buka stared into the darkened fireplace again.

"I remember the time you decide you goin' to the island. Your Mistress send you to deliver a message to Mistress Phillips. You deliver the message an' then decide you runnin' away to the island."

Obi sighed. "Yes, I remember." He was impatient for an answer, but he knew Buka rarely gave a simple yes or no.

"Good thing I catch you walkin' down that road—you goin' west and the island be east." He chuckled. "You have to know whether the road you choose is the right one."

He turned away from the fireplace and faced Obi. "S'pose she ain't there no more?"

"Then I keep goin' to Mexico," Obi said softly. "This way I don't be thinkin' she still there waitin'."

"You can't do nothin' without careful plan. That's how you be on the wrong road before. I hear Jeremiah put the box on the horse and point the horse south. He ride north. People say you go to the Yankee an' you be free."

Obi jumped up like a rabbit. "It true, Buka?"

Buka shrugged his frail shoulders. "Is only what I hear.

But while the white men in confusion, this may be the best time to run."

Obi was both frightened and excited by the idea. He sat down in front of Buka again and told him how John Jennings was becoming like Wilson.

"Course they alike," Buka said. "They brothers. Same as them North men an' these whites down here."

"But they killin' each other," Obi said.

"Brothers do that sometime. They's a lot of funerals 'cause of that Virginny battle. Tyler Phillips ain't the only one bury today."

Absentmindedly, Obi watched a spider building a web in the corner over the fireplace. "I want run now, Buka. 'Specially since Wilson home for good."

"We have to make careful plan. Go back. I come to the barn tonight. Don't make nobody suspicious."

Obi left the shack and picked his way quickly over the small stones and brambles beside the creek. He stopped to take a drink of water. Suddenly, he felt happy and excited. The blue, cloudless sky and the cold, fresh water added to his joy. It was a perfect day—perfect for a picnic! He'd get Easter and Jason and they'd pick some peaches and get the rest of the corn bread. They'd have a feast and wash it all down with clabber, a kind of milk they sometimes drank that had a thick, rich curd. Then they'd rest in the shade of the oak grove.

He was still thinking about the picnic when he walked into the yard. Wilson faced him there with his thick, black belt wrapped around his fist. "Where you been?" he yelled.

Four

When the war came along I was a grown man, and I went off to serve because Old Master was too old to go, but he had to send somebody anyways.

George Kye, ex-slave
From *Voices from Slavery*

Obi's first instinct was to run, but he hesitated when he saw Jason sobbing nearby, curled up in a ball on the ground. Easter was still in the field. Wilson grabbed Obi by the neck of his shirt. "Where you been?"he yelled again.

"Went to check on a sow I thought was loose, suh," he said, avoiding Wilson's eyes.

"You lyin'!" The muscles in Wilson's thick neck stood out as if they would burst through his skin. Obi could have kicked himself for not guessing that Wilson wouldn't stay at the funeral.

Still clutching him, Wilson drew back his free hand and snapped the strap across Obi's leg. Obi grabbed Wilson's shoulder, digging his fingers in the back of his neck. Jason, still sobbing, scrambled up from the ground. Stumbling frantically into the wheelbarrow, he sent it toppling over. Wilson ripped Obi's shirt down the front as Obi jerked away from him, trying to grab Wilson's upraised hand. Obi couldn't get a grip on him, and Wilson lashed the strap across Obi's cheek.

Wilson drew back his hand to hit Obi again but stopped short at the sound of horses' hooves in the yard.

"Mornin', sir," a voice said.

Wilson loosened his grip. Obi, breathing heavily, backed away from Wilson and almost fell on top of Jason, who was still sprawled over the wheelbarrow. Jason sat up, his face wet and dirty. They stared at the two soldiers.

Both soldiers wore the same grey tunics and soft forage caps. One of them had a smooth, boyish face. The other looked older and wore a thick, black mustache. The one with the mustache dismounted. "I'm Captain Clark. How're y'all this mornin'?" he asked brightly.

"Mornin'," Wilson mumbled. There was a bright red spot on his neck where Obi had grabbed him. He gave Obi a warning look. Jason wiped his eyes with the back of his hands, and Obi still trembled as he glared at the red blotch on Wilson's neck.

"This the Jennings farm?" the captain asked.

"Yes," Wilson answered. He tried to fold his belt in his hand.

The captain rubbed his mustache. "These some difficult times, sir," he said. "People 'round here been good about helpin' us." He glanced at Obi and Jason. "How many Negroes y'all have?"

Wilson pointed to Obi. "He the only field hand. The other two is children. That runt and a gal."

The captain rubbed his mustache again, while the other soldier, still astride his horse, took notes in a small book.

"Seems to be a sufficient farm," Captain Clark said.

"It'll do," Wilson frowned. "Barely scratchin' a livin' out of it."

"How many acres?"

Wilson spread his stout legs as if he were balancing himself on a ship. "Twenty. Who wants all this information?"

"The government. Because of the war, everybody's had to help."

"I hope y'all ain't lookin' for no man old as me to go marchin' off to war," Wilson said.

The captain smiled slightly and rubbed his mustache again. "Well, sir, not exactly. People are aidin' us whichever way they can. And that's why we ask questions. So's we don't ask for what people can't give, sir. You have a wife and children?"

Obi slowly grew calmer as he listened to Wilson answer the captain's questions.

"We need soldiers, provisions, slaves—whatever can be spared." The captain stared at Obi.

"We can't spare nothin'," Wilson said loudly.

Captain Clark walked toward Obi. "You don't mind, sir, if I take a look at him?" he said.

"Suit yourself," Wilson answered and put his belt around his waist.

The captain put his hand on Obi's shoulder. "Open your mouth," he said curtly.

Obi opened his mouth and the captain checked his gums and teeth for signs of disease. He pulled up Obi's ripped shirt, inspecting his skin for open sores, then squeezed Obi's arms and legs.

The inspection reminded Obi of the way John Jennings checked mules before he bought them.

Captain Clark turned to the other soldier. "Clean, healthy, strong, prime. About fifteen or sixteen," he said. The soldier wrote quickly.

Wilson seemed ready to explode. He leaned into the captain's face. "He's the only field hand we got. How we goin' to get our crop in? How we goin' to live through the winter, Captain?" he shouted.

The captain sighed, lowering his voice as Wilson spoke louder.

"We're all fightin' the same cause. People been donatin' their slaves."

"I ain't got a hundred slaves. We ain't no rich slaveholders!" he yelled.

"We're fightin' so you keep what you have. We don't want you to lose none of this." He waved his hands toward the fields.

Wilson stared at Jason, whose round eyes were still fearful. "That one is useless. You take him," he said, pointing at Obi, "and we done for. We don't have no one else in the field." No sooner had the words left Wilson's mouth than Easter walked into the yard leading the mule.

"She's in the field," the captain said firmly.

"She ain't no real hand. Not much better in the field than the runt."

Easter looked at Obi.

"Don't stand there with your mouth open," Wilson said to her. "Empty them sacks and get back to work."

Captain Clark watched as Easter went into the barn, still leading the mule. "Sir, we're all makin' sacrifices. Some are givin' their lives. We're only askin' for one nigger to serve a year." He smiled sweetly at Wilson. "We have to build breastworks near Charleston. Takes a lot of manpower to put up those walls. He'll be goin' to Charleston, sir, but he's still your property."

Obi's heart raced. He thought about Tyler, who was dead, and Jeremiah, who was probably dead also. He looked down at his bare feet, not wanting anyone to guess his thoughts. *It time to run now.*

The captain mounted his horse. "We'll return in three weeks, sir. Give you time to get your croppin' done."

Obi kept his face down. When they came back in three weeks, he'd be gone.

"Guess we ain't got no say in the matter!" Wilson said angrily, raising his voice.

The captain ignored his comment. "What else you grow besides tobacco?"

The other soldier pulled out his notebook again.

"Tobacco's our big crop."

"Maybe you could also spare a hog or two and a few bushels of corn, peas—whatever—for our sons? The boys are sacrificin' their lives." He saluted Wilson. "Three weeks, sir."

They rode out of the yard. Easter, looking frightened, left the barn.

Obi clenched his fist, expecting Wilson to fly into a rage again. He knew he'd have to pay for what he'd done, but a part of him was glad that he'd tried to fight back.

Wilson kept his belt around his waist. "Get back in that field," he yelled at Easter. Then, turning to Obi, he said stonily, "You let that gal work alone. You crop in Master John's field."

Jason gazed at Wilson in fear as if he were expecting to be hit again.

"You collect the firewood," he said to the small boy gruffly.

Obi's head pounded as he, Wilson, and Easter walked back to the fields. Wilson swaggered a few feet ahead of them. Glancing at the cool, green oak grove, Obi felt as if he had the great iron shackles around his ankles again—like those he'd worn when they came off the boats in Charleston Harbor.

The sun burned directly overhead. Normally it would be about time for their midday meal. This usually consisted of whatever was left over from the previous evening's meal, and they'd eat right out in the field.

But Obi knew now that Wilson wouldn't let them stop working long enough to drink a cup of water. Easter, walking close to him, held his hand. Obi knew she had a million questions to ask, but Wilson was close enough to hear anything they said.

"I tell you later what happen," he whispered to her as they parted. She and Wilson cropped in the same field. *Makin' sure she don't take a minute rest,* Obi told himself. When he reached the farthest field, he sat down among the tall tobacco stalks, knowing that Wilson couldn't see him. He held his throbbing head for a few moments before beginning work. When he felt a little better, he worked steadily, leading his mule back and forth along the rows of wide green leaves.

As soon as his sacks were full, he led the mule out of the field and saw Easter in the distance working side by side with Wilson. While Obi emptied the leaves in the barn, he heard John and Martha's wagon rattle into the yard. He was relieved that they were back.

He also heard Wilson calling to his brother. Instead of rushing back out into the hot sun, Obi took a few minutes to bundle a pile of leaves. Wilson came into the yard and started talking, but Obi couldn't tell what he was saying.

After tying the leaves, Obi left the barn. Wilson and Master John were waiting for him. Martha Jennings, in her somber black dress and bonnet, stood behind the men. Her long, thin face looked weary and blank.

Jason, staggering under an armful of wood, stumbled into the yard. He almost dropped the wood when he saw Martha. "Mistress, I—"

She put her finger to her lips. "Take that wood in the shed and go bring Easter here," Jennings ordered. "And bring me some rope."

Jason walked unsteadily around the barn to the shed and then ran off for Easter. Obi started to lead the mule back to the field. "You wait here!" Master John said sternly. Jennings's high, sharp cheekbones protruded out of his face like two pieces of granite.

Obi's hands became wet and clammy. He tried to form the words in his head so that he could tell his side of the story—mainly, that he grabbed Wilson without even thinking.

He didn't look at Wilson standing next to his brother, but he caught Martha's eyes for a moment. Though she didn't say anything, a softness in her look told him that *she* understood how he felt.

When Easter and Jason walked into the yard, Master John glared at the three of them. Jason handed him the rope. "When I tell y'all to stay on this land, I mean it!"

"I wasn't doin' nothin' wrong, Master John," Obi protested. His wide nostrils flared slightly.

"You wasn't workin' when you was supposed to, and you put a hand on my brother. Some would beat you to an inch of your life for that. Some would even kill you," he said, never taking his eyes off Obi.

Wilson started removing his belt as John turned to him. "Twenty-five lashes. Give the other two five apiece."

Easter and Martha both gasped, and Jason looked as if he were ready to fly out of the yard.

Martha stepped up to her husband, clutching his arm. "Give them extra work, or don't feed them tonight, but don't beat on them," she pleaded.

He pulled his arm away from her. "Hush, woman. You the one who spoiled them."

Martha clenched her teeth and walked quickly into the house, slamming the door behind her. Wilson grinned with narrowed eyes at Obi. "Take your shirt off and stand under that tree."

Obi silently obeyed him and stepped under the beautiful magnolia. Master John tied Obi's hands around the tree. Jason was already sobbing as he buried his head against Easter's thigh. Easter put her arms around him and stared into space.

Wilson raised his arm. "This is what happens when you put your hands on a white man." The cracking sound the belt made when it hit Obi's flesh seemed to echo throughout the farm. Obi bit his lips until they bled, but he would not cry out. He wanted to scream—the way his mother had screamed—but each time the belt cut his flesh, he kept one thought in mind: *I put a mark on you too, Wilson.*

Easter heard the lashes but never watched. She gazed at the blue sky and tried to listen to the songs of the brownish-gray mockingbirds. Jason kept his head buried in her dress.

When Wilson finished, Master John untied Obi. He slid slowly to the ground.

Easter made a movement toward him, but Wilson grabbed

her by the wrist. He whacked her five times on her legs with the belt. Her eyes filled with tears that spilled over, but she made no sound. Jason also took five lashes, with his arms wrapped around Easter's small waist and his face hidden against her stomach.

Obi watched Wilson beating them. His inability to help Easter and Jason hurt him more than his own lashing.

"These is war times and people is dyin'. I ain't goin' to have y'all comin' and goin' as you please," Master John warned. "Everybody git back to work. Jason, you better stop crying 'fore I give you somethin' to cry about. You go in the field with Easter and Obi. And you work. Don't want to see you just totin' water all day."

Wilson had a satisfied look on his face. He watched as Easter helped Obi to his feet and the three children trudged to the fields.

Jason clung tightly to Easter's hand as they walked. The sun burned into the welts that were beginning to rise on Obi's back. When they were hidden among the tall tobacco stalks, Obi sat on the ground and Easter sank to her knees and looked at his bleeding back.

She embraced him around his waist, and he buried his face in her neck. They both cried. Jason stood next to them, patting Obi's shoulders tenderly and sniffling loudly. They stayed there for a time, drawing comfort from one another.

Then the stalks parted and the three of them jumped. Martha, face drawn and her lips set in a thin line, handed Easter clean rags and a bucket of water.

She wore her field dress and the bonnet that she wore while she worked.

"Mistress, why Master let Wilson beat us?" Easter asked tearfully.

"Git to work before Wilson comes," Martha said. "We'll talk later."

"Thank you, Mistress," Obi said softly as she left.

Easter wet one of the rags in the water and dabbed it on

Obi's back. "I didn't tell on you, Obi," Jason whimpered.

Obi winced when Easter touched an open welt. "I know. It ain't your fault."

Jason's little face was twisted with worry. "Wilson snuck up on me. Ask what I doin'. I tell him I makin' sure that old sow ain't 'round here." Sounding hurt and confused, he asked, "Why Master John let Wilson beat us?"

"Somethin's terrible wrong, little Jason," Easter said. Obi stood up when she finished. She took another rag and cleaned Jason's dirty face and legs.

"Take my mule an' work this row. I talk to Easter a minute," Obi said to Jason.

Jason stroked the animal as it moved down the row of stalks.

"Easter, I ain't waitin' for them soldiers to come get me."

"What you do, then?"

"Get away from here."

""You runnin'?"she whispered, looking frightened and as if she might cry.

He nodded.

She stared at the ground. "What about me an' Jason?" she asked.

Obi looked toward the house and spotted Wilson walking toward them.

"Here Wilson come. Talk later."

Five

No sooner had the armies, East and West, penetrated Virginia
and Tennessee than fugitive slaves appeared within their lines.

Dr. W.E.B. Du Bois
From *The Souls of Black Folk*

When the sun set, Obi took the mule to the barn for the
last time that day. He and Jason finished their chores and
cleaned themselves, then Jason went to the kitchen.

Obi needed to think and calm himself. He threaded the
needle Easter had just sent with Jason and stitched his shirt.

As always, when he was afraid or lonely, he tried to
remember his mother's face. He could remember her screams,
but he had to picture her face as Buka had described it to
him. As he sewed, he tried to put his mind to his usual
fantasy about running away and finding her, but other im-
ages clouded this vision.

Instead, he thought about the runaways he'd seen brought
back to the Phillips plantation after they were caught by
the patterollers. The patterollers were men who policed the
countryside. They usually beat up a runaway before he or
she was returned to the owner.

The excitement Obi had felt earlier was gone, beaten
out of him by Wilson. Yet he'd survived Wilson's lashes.
Could the patterollers be any worse?

Easter, calling him from the yard, startled him out of his thoughts. He left the barn and walked to the house for supper. Martha Jennings stayed in the kitchen while they ate. The creases in her long, narrow face seemed deeper than usual. Obi wished she'd hurry and leave so that he could talk to Easter privately. The voices of the men sounded like a distant rumbling from the sitting room.

Martha picked up the ladle, dropped it, and then knocked a wooden plate off the sideboard.

"Got to git an early start tomorrow," she said. Her voice was shrill.

"Yes, um," Easter mumbled, giving Obi a puzzled look. Easter and Jason slept on the floor in the kitchen and were always the first ones up. They wondered what she was talking about.

Easter's frown lines appeared on her forehead as she took a spoonful of rice and cowpeas. She'd taken off her field dress and wore the only other clothing she had—another homespun dress worn under a long apron.

Martha sat at her spinning wheel, which was near the fireplace. "Still need cloth. Might as well work a while. Easter, when you and Jason finish eatin', come help me with this spinnin'."

The children looked at one another. Normally, she'd be in the room with the men and start her spinning after the three of them had finished eating and the kitchen was cleaned.

After they had cleared the kitchen, Jason got the wire carding brushes for cleaning and combing the cotton before it was spun.

Obi walked to the door. He couldn't speak to Easter now, so he'd decided to go to the barn and wait for Buka.

Martha looked at him sadly. "Obi, you stay on here with us. Don't you have tools to fix? Or you want to carve some wood? You can do it here."

"Mistress, I go in the barn."

"Stay with us." Her voice cracked slightly as her leg

moved up and down, treadling the wheel. "Need to stay together as much as we can now." Her soft brown eyes were wet.

She look the same way the day Jason's mother die, Obi thought. He recalled how surprised he had been at the way she cried over the dead black woman.

Easter put down her carding brush. "Mistress, what's the matter?"

Martha looked at each of them, brushing the back of her hand across her eyes. She spoke in a whisper. "Y'all let on I told you this, I'll whip you myself. They're sellin' the farm and they're sellin' y'all. We're movin' west. We're gettin' away from this war if we can."

There was no doubt in Obi's mind now. He had to run. Jason's face was blank. Easter was the only one who spoke. "Mistress, we be sold together?" she asked, trying to sound brave.

Martha shook her head. "Don't be foolish, girl. Master John'll get a good price for you at Master Phillips's. You could be a cook, or a seamstress, or a nurse, or even a ladies' maid. You're a smart, pretty gal. Mistress Phillips will be glad to have you."

She treadled the wheel furiously. "You learn fast. There ain't nothin' you can't do. Some of the things I showed you, you do better than me now."

Martha stopped spinning and the tears rolled down her flat cheeks. "You, Obi. They're goin' to sell you in the Charleston market. You're worth maybe one thousand dollars, young and strong as you are. They're sellin' you first. Before the soldiers come back."

She reached down and rubbed Jason's small, round head. "And you ain't nothin' but a peck of corn, boy. I don't know what we'll do with you. Only thing you know how to do is sing pretty. Maybe get fifty dollars for you—somewheres."

Jason slowly grasped what she was saying. "Don't want you to sell me, Mistress," he whined. Easter stared at nothing in particular and shook her head. Martha continued.

"Missy Holmes is gettin' married. Maybe we'll give you to her for a weddin' present." She looked again at Obi. "So you see, we better sit here together, because we goin' to be separated soon."

Obi paced impatiently from one end of the barn to the other while waiting for Buka to arrive. He hoped Buka hadn't come and left while he was in the kitchen. It was important that he talk with him tonight. Wilson and Master John were selling him. By tomorrow night or the next, he had to be on his way.

He opened the barn door to see if a lantern still burned in the house. If Buka didn't come to the barn, then he would go to the shack. The moon was full and bright, but the house was dark. Obi closed the door, wondering what to do, and the hounds stirred, wagging their tails. Easter rushed into the barn. "Have to speak to you," she said. She sat under the hayloft on the milking stool. Obi sat cross-legged in front of her on the floor.

"Take me an' Jason with you when you run."

"I can't take you an' Jason," Obi said. "It too dangerous, an' how we get anywhere with him?"

"I take care of him." She took one of Obi's long, calloused hands in hers. "We always been together, Obi."

His fantasy about running had never included Easter and Jason. Now that he was faced with the reality of actually leaving, he realized that Easter was right—over the years, they had become a part of him.

He rubbed his forehead. "Maybe I go hide in the woods a while. I could keep a eye on you an' Jason. If you sold to Master Phillips, I could come back for you."

"What about Jason?"

"If he give or sold to Missy Holmes, we find him easy."

He felt her hand tremble slightly. "If we separate now, then we never see each other again," she said, trying to keep her voice steady. "Remember you tell me one time we was like family—all we had was each other?"

"Sometimes even families have to separate. When them two—Joseph and Pat—on the Phillips place run, they leave their children," Obi said.

"I hear they comin' back for them."

"I'll come back for you an' Jason. After I find my way to Mexico."

"If we don't leave together, we ain't gonna see each other again, Obi."

"It ain't possible to leave together—Jason too much of a baby, for one thing."

"I told you I see to Jason."

Obi's throat tightened. He was glad he couldn't see her determined face. He'd miss her—miss both of them. He thought of the little, scared, barefoot girl wearing a shirttail made out of sacking. Wilson brought her to the farm on an Easter Sunday as a gift for Martha. She wouldn't stop crying until Obi thought to give her some molasses candy.

She ain't no more little girl, he realized. Suddenly, he wanted to tell her about his dream, and for the first time he shared with someone besides Buka his desire to find his mother.

Easter was quiet a moment when Obi finished talking. "I don't have no remembrance of nothin' except livin' here. You an' Jason my family. Take us with you an' we help you find your ma."

A pebble hit the barn door and Obi stood up. The dogs whined and wagged their tails. "That's Buka," Obi said, relieved, as he opened the door. Easter made space for the old man under the hayloft as Obi placed a crate there for him to sit on.

Buka was silent for a few minutes after Obi told him about the soldiers' visit and the family selling the farm.

"This war bring confusion," he said at last. "Now the time to run. The blacksmith from Master Phillips' place come see me today. He say black people runnin' off the plantations and escapin' to the Yankee soldier."

Easter's voice came quietly out of the shadows. "You think me an' Jason can run too?"

Obi broke in before the old man could answer. "I move fast alone. I just hide in the woods. Between me an' you, Buka, we keep a eye on Easter an' Jason."

Buka coughed. "I take all of you to the Sea islands. Big rice plantations with more African than white man. I still have friends an' people there who hide an' protect you. They help you make your way north. Wilson never find you."

"An' we stay together," Easter muttered.

Buka stood up stiffly. "Tomorrow, soon as the family sleep, meet me at the creek."

"When the clock ring nine times they all in bed," Easter said.

"Anything we have to carry?" Obi asked.

"I take care of all that. I get britches for Jason an' Easter an' other things we need."

"Britches?" Easter said.

"Dress you like a boy. Jennings put out advertisement for you as a girl. If we caught, it better that patterollers think you a boy."

Buka shuffled slowly toward the door, and Obi wondered how far the old man would be able to travel. "How long it take to get to the Sea islands?" Obi asked.

"Three nights." He cleared his throat. "Easter, Obi, come close. Tomorrow at nine, you be sure to come to the creek. Now, this important. If we stopped by patteroller, we say we goin' to a funeral at Brantley's farm. I get pass."

"Suppose Wilson or Master John catch us—we tell them that too?" Obi asked.

"Don't say nothin' about funeral or the farm to them. Only say that to the patteroller if they run up on us." He paused. "If Master John beat you till you faint, say nothin'."

"I know when they all sleep," Easter said. "Master and

Wilson snore to wake the dead. They sleep fast these days too, from bein' in the field."

Buka placed his hands on both their shoulders. "You make sure Wilson an' Master John don't catch you leavin'."

The old man opened the door. Round-shouldered and shriveled, he seemed to disappear into the hedges. Easter followed him, her bare feet gliding lightly over the pebbles.

Obi closed the barn door and climbed into the hayloft. After dreaming so long of escape, the time had finally come. He still felt uneasy about taking Easter and Jason—especially Jason. But Buka was leading them. That should make the trip less difficult and dangerous.

Obi was up the next morning before dawn after a fitful sleep. He and Easter decided at breakfast not to tell Jason anything until it was time to leave. Easter did warn Jason, however, not to do anything that day to anger Wilson or Master John.

As the day wore on, Obi hoped Buka was able to get everything they needed for the trip. Probably someone at the plantation would give Buka clothing and food. He wondered, though, how Buka would obtain a pass.

Easter and Obi worked hard, not wanting to do anything to arouse suspicion.

As soon as the sun set behind the oak grove, Obi wanted to take off across the fields and go to the creek, but he had to wait. Wearily he led the mule to the barn, with Wilson leading the other mule behind him.

At the barn entrance, Wilson left his mule for Obi to take inside and empty the sacks.

Jason brought in the cows while Obi unharnessed the mules. After he put the cows in their stalls, the boy climbed up to the hayloft and threw down hay for the animals. He worked without his usual chatter.

Wilson came to the barn door and broke the silence. "We're takin' the tobacco to Phillips tonight, after supper."

"Yes, suh," Obi said, trying not to show any emotion.

Though he knew they could get to the plantation and return to the farm in more than enough time to meet Buka, this sudden change in their routine bothered him. Usually they took the tobacco to the plantation in the morning.

He tried to stay calm as he helped Wilson hitch the wagons to the mules and load the leaves. Maybe Wilson only wanted to make sure they didn't miss any time in the field tomorrow.

Jason jumped out of the hayloft, his eyes asking what his mouth was afraid to. Obi asked for him. "Can Jason come with us, suh?"

"No." Wilson looked at Jason. "Finish feedin' them animals." Jason scrambled back into the hayloft.

When Obi went to supper, Martha Jennings stayed in the kitchen again while they ate. Her face was hidden as she bent over her mending.

"Mistress, I help you," Easter called from the table. "Why don't you wait till we finish eat?"

"Don't fret about me," Martha said.

Obi took a piece of corn bread, but he was too nervous to eat.

"We takin' the tobacco to the plantation," he said to Easter.

She looked worried. "Tonight?"

"Master Wilson say I can't go," Jason whined.

Martha started to say something to Jason, but Wilson came into the kitchen. "Let's move on," he ordered. Obi got up from the table.

Jason helped Easter stack the wooden plates.

"Come on, I ain't got time for all that," Wilson said to Easter. He nodded in Jason's direction. "Let him clean."

At first, Easter didn't realize that Wilson was talking to her.

"Yes, suh?" she said, looking confused.

"You're comin' too."

Easter dropped the plates on the table and turned to Martha. Martha rose quickly from her chair, visibly trembling. "You and Obi are goin' to the Phillipses' to hire out as field hands for their cotton crop."

Easter looked as if she were about to cry. "Mistress, what about the tobacco croppin'?"

"We'll finish that ourselves. Most of it's done now." The shirt Martha was mending fell unnoticed to the floor. "They hirin' you out early. Don't want to lose money."

Wilson gave Martha a disgusted look and waited in the doorway.

"What about me, Mistress?" Jason's frightened eyes filled with tears.

"Boy, you're too young to hire out," she said.

Easter went over to Martha. She clutched her arm. "Mistress, why we have to go now? We never hire out this early—"

"Gal, what's wrong with you?" Wilson yelled angrily. "Come on!"

Obi pulled Easter away. "Come on, Easter. We go now."

Six

Not only will we abstain from all interferences with your slaves, but we will, with an iron hand, crush any attempt at insurrection on their part.

From the Proclamation to
the People of Western Virginia,
May 26, 1861
General George B. McClellan, Union Army

Easter put her arms around Jason's shoulders as they watched Obi bring the mules with the wagons out of the barn. "We see you soon, Jason. Don't cry, now," she said, wiping his face. The hot, humid air was heavy.

"You an' Obi comin' back?"

She bent down and kissed him on his forehead, her voice cracking. "We be back—soon." Easter climbed behind Obi on one of the mules, and Wilson mounted the other. Jason waved, his small mouth quivering as he tried not to cry. Martha came out of the kitchen and stood behind him. Easter waved and looked back until she could no longer see Jason and Martha in the gathering dusk.

Obi knew that this was the last they'd see of the Jennings farm. He didn't know how, but they'd get to Buka tonight.

"I know somethin' go wrong, Obi," Easter said softly. "I feel it all day." She held him tightly around his waist. Because of the wagon clanging noisily down the road, their words were hidden from Wilson, who rode behind.

"How we get to the creek now?" she asked.

"We find some way. Now I see why Wilson rush us to work so hard."

Easter squirmed. "We never work in the field at Master Phillips." She sighed. "Obi, it take three week for the cotton crop to be pick. This way they make some of the money they would from hirin' us out in the winter."

"They have us sold before the soldiers come back," Obi said. His head swirled. He had no idea how they'd be able to sneak off the closely guarded plantation. "Maybe we find someone there who help us get to Buka. Or who tell Buka where we are."

"But we have to get Jason too," she reminded him.

He hadn't thought about Jason. "We have to sneak back in the house to do that. Get caught for sure." The road began to widen, and he sensed Wilson moving up to ride alongside. "We talk later," he whispered.

They rode the rest of the way in silence. The closer they got to George Phillips's three hundred acres of land, the more determined Obi became to find a way to leave.

When they rode through the gates of the plantation, they saw a group of men standing on the lawn. George Phillips was talking with them.

"They soldiers?" Easter asked.

Obi strained to see. "I think so." He thought he recognized the grey Confederate caps. Normally, their wagons would have been met at the gate by one of Phillips's people. Tonight, however, small groups of slaves watched the men talking, keeping a careful distance from them. Phillips's face was as somber as his black suit.

"What the devil's going on?" Wilson mumbled.

When they climbed off their mules, Jessie, the overseer who'd brought the news about Tyler, spotted them. He walked across the lawn.

"Hello, sir," he said to Wilson. Then he motioned with his hand toward the soldiers. "The family see so much trouble—now this."

Wilson placed his hand on the mule's neck. "What happened?"

Jessie shook his head. "Jeremiah try and run off to them Yankees instead a watchin' out for young Tyler like he supposed to." He spread his thin mouth in a grin. "But them Yankees trick him. Send him right back here. Tell our soldiers that they ain't fightin' this war to steal nobody's property."

Obi's heart raced as he stared at the cluster of men on the lawn. Now he recognized a tall figure, his hands tied behind his back. *Jeremiah!* he said to himself. He and Easter glanced at each other. She too realized what this meant: Running to Yankee soldiers wasn't the way to freedom.

Obi wished he could talk to Jeremiah—find out what his plan had been and why it hadn't worked. Wilson and Jessie started toward the tobacco barn. Obi and Easter followed, leading the mules. As they passed the soldiers, Obi tried to catch Jeremiah's eyes, but Jeremiah's head was thrown back. He looked defiant, standing straight and tall and seeming to stare at the dark, starless sky.

"That boy goin' to suffer now," Jessie said. "Master Phillips don't allow no beatin' 'less someone real bad, and that's a bad one."

Wilson spat on the ground. "Wish I was back on the sea. Sick to death of war—sick to death of slaves and dirt."

They passed the smokehouse, where meat was cured and stored. Obi tried to block out the men's conversation so that he could think. He had to figure out a way to meet Buka—tonight!

They walked by the spinning house, and Obi heard the women inside laughing and talking softly as they spun the cotton thread that would be woven into cloth. It was a familiar sound, and comforting at a time when things were changing rapidly. He would have liked to stay there and listen a while longer.

When they reached the tobacco barn, a young woman came out to help unload the leaves from the wagons. As soon as one of the wagons was empty, Wilson turned to Jessie. "I'll be back tomorrow for that other wagon and mule," he said.

Obi wished he could take the mule himself and ride away with Easter.

"You stay in the long cabin tonight," Jessie said to Obi.

Obi looked surprised. "I ain't stayin' with Thomas, suh?"

"You workin' in the field, not with the carpenter."

"Suh, I thought I could stay with Thomas in the cabin." Obi kept after the overseer because he didn't want to be in the long cabin with a lot of other men.

"You stay where you told to stay," Wilson told him. He turned to Jessie. "He give you any trouble, you put him on that whippin' post. Watch him good."

The overseer winked. "He'll be safe here."

Obi felt trapped as he took another bundle of tobacco to the barn. It would be almost impossible to get away without the help of one of the Phillips people. Though he knew many of the slaves, he didn't know if he could trust any. Who would help him without turning him in before he even got to Buka?

"The gal can stay in the nursery," Jessie told Wilson. The nursery was a cabin for children who had no mothers. During the day it was used for the babies belonging to the women who worked in the fields. They were cared for while their mothers worked. Two old women who could no longer labor as field hands took care of the children.

Easter stared at the ground. Usually she stayed with the cook's helper in a small shed behind the kitchen of the family house.

Wilson got on the mule and rode off without looking back. The women who had been working in the barn were leaving. "Y'all go on to the cabins," Jessie said to Obi and Easter. "Curfew startin' now, and the horn will be blowin' at five in the mornin'."

He walked away from them, heading in the direction of the far pasture. Obi guessed that he was going to find out what was happening to Jeremiah, who was by now probably in the plantation jail, on the outskirts of the property.

As soon as the overseer was out of earshot, the women began to talk. One of them put her hands on Easter's shoulders.

"Why you here in July?" She didn't wait for an answer but continued talking. "You see they bring Jeremiah back?" They started walking toward the cabins.

"Jeremiah a fool," a short woman walking next to Obi said, "believin' them stories he hear about soldiers comin' to free us."

The large, white, two-story plantation house loomed over them as they passed it on their way to the slave quarters. The lawn was clear of people now. Behind the house, a footpath bordered with cypress and magnolia trees led away from the house. Easter was on the verge of tears as they approached the quarters. There were two rows of one-room log cabins that faced each other—seventeen on each side of a narrow path.

People sat talking in front of and in the narrow alleys between the cabins. Some of them sat around small fires. Ordinarily, by now most of them would be inside after the grueling field work. They'd eat, do their chores, and sleep early. Though barely a sound could be heard, Obi guessed they were talking about Jeremiah.

The women who had walked with Easter and Obi joined different groups of people. Obi put his arm around Easter's shoulders.

"We find a way," he said. "Buka ain't gonna leave without us. He leavin' to show us the way. Otherwise he stay right here."

Easter gazed at the small fires and the people huddled around them. "I don't like stayin' in these cabin. I could be with Rose in the shed or at the farm with Jason and Mistress."

Obi sighed. "Wherever you be, you still a slave. I don't

like it either. My mind made up. We figure a way to leave."

"And get Jason too!"

"Go on to the cabin now," Obi said, ignoring her comment.

Obi watched her disappear into the shadows as she walked to the nursery at the end of the rows of cabins. He didn't know how they could get Jason. He didn't dislike the boy, but he wasn't going to jeopardize his own chances of running in order to save a child.

Jason hardly know he in slavery, he told himself. *Someday Jason be a man an' free he own self.* As he walked to the long cabin, he realized that everyone was outside—even the children, who weren't playing but sitting quietly with the adults.

A group of men sat around a fire. They stopped talking when Obi approached. All the men knew Obi, but only one, a man called Julius, greeted him. Though Julius made room for him in the circle, Obi sensed that he was unwelcome.

"What you doin' here in July?" Julius asked.

"I here for the cotton."

"You ain't workin' with the carpenter?" Julius said, surprised.

Obi shook his head. "Easter here too. She in the nursery."

"Guess your master finish he own croppin'?" Julius said.

Obi wanted to say, "Ain't got no master," but Buka had taught him to keep silent. *Trust no one with your secrets unless they takin' the same chances you is,* Buka had said.

Obi nodded in response to Julius's question and wondered whether there was anyone in the quiet, secretive circle of men who'd help him get to Buka.

Sensing someone staring at him, Obi turned away from Julius and looked straight in the eyes of Rayford, George Phillips's personal servant. The proud, arrogant man was one of the Phillips' most favored slaves and was called

"Massa Rayford" behind his back. Obi had never known him to associate with any of the other slaves. He even had his own small room in the family house.

But on this night, instead of the clean, white trousers and shirt he usually wore, Rayford had on a rough, home-spun shirt and overalls like the field hands. His dark eyes jumped and flickered in the firelight. He was staring angrily at Obi. Then he stood quickly. The others rose with him. Obi looked from one man to the other, wondering what he'd done wrong.

"You can go to the cabin," Julius said to Obi. "There be a pallet under the shutter. You can sleep there."

Obi had the feeling that the men were going somewhere. Why would Rayford be there, dressed like a hand?

"You goin' inside too?" Obi asked.

"Yes," Julius said, but he hesitated. Obi knew he was lying—the other men had already slipped away—so he stayed where he was.

Rayford snuffed out the fire. Then he grabbed Obi by the shoulders. "What you want?" he asked gruffly. "What they send you here for?" he added.

Obi tried to pull himself out of the larger man's grip. "The overseer tell me to sleep in the long cabin." He knew for certain now that the men were planning something. Maybe this was an opportunity for him to get help. He tried to remain calm. "Master hire me out early—but I supposed to meet Buka tonight."

Rayford's grip loosened, and Obi noticed that Julius seemed interested when he said Buka's name. He took a chance.

"Can you show me how to get to Buka?" he asked.

"It dangerous, Obi," Julius said nervously. "Patterollers come right here, an' the dogs is let out too. One side the patterollers, an' the other side the dogs. Just go in the cabin, Obi, like you supposed to," he said softly.

"Tell me where the dogs be—I take my chance with them," Obi pleaded.

"What business you have with Buka?" Rayford whispered hoarsely.

Obi decided to gamble once more. "Buka takin' me an' Easter to a funeral at Brantley's farm."

Rayford grabbed Obi's arm and pushed him in the cabin. Obi twisted and tried to speak, "Rayford, suh, I—"

"Quiet," he ordered.

Obi's head pounded so hard he thought he'd faint. He should never have mentioned the funeral. Julius followed them into the cabin, empty of men. "Light a candle," Rayford told Julius.

When the candle was lit, Rayford knelt on the floor near one of the pallets. He quickly loosened an area of dirt with a hoe and pulled out a tin box. He looked at Obi. "What you say the girl's name is?"

"Easter," Obi mumbled. His hands were clammy as he tried to figure out what was happening.

"She in the nursery," Julius informed Rayford.

"Get her," Rayford ordered him.

Julius left the cabin and Obi tried to explain. "Rayford, suh, I—"

Rayford held up his hand. "No time for a lot of talk." He opened the tin box and took out a pen, ink, and parchment. To Obi's amazement, he began to write in a beautiful hand:

Permission is granted to Obi and Easter to attend the funeral at the farm of D. Brantley on the evening of July 27, 1861, and return to the Phillips plantation by ten p.m.

Signed: George Phillips

Rayford folded the note and handed it to Obi. "In case we're stopped," he said. *This where Buka get he pass,* Obi realized. Rayford placed the box back in the hole and carefully covered it over with dirt. "I thought you was sent to spy. You usually with that carpenter, and he love the ground ol' Master step on."

It seemed strange to Obi to hear loyal Rayford speak so disrespectfully about George Phillips. He smiled. "Thank you for the pass. How you learn to read an' write? I ask Mistress once to teach me—she say it against the law."

Rayford's stern face softened as he continued to pack the dirt over the box. "She probably can't read or write herself. Tyler taught me. When I take him back an' forth to school, I tell him, 'Show me what you learn today.' "

Rayford stood up. "But I never let on that I learn. I always say, 'You a smart boy, Tyler. Dumb Rayford can't catch that at all.' The boy taught me everything he knew, God bless his soul." Rayford laughed.

When they left the cabin, Easter was waiting with Julius outside. She rushed over to Obi. "What happened?"

"We meetin' Buka," he said happily, expecting her to share his excitement.

"But what about Jason?"

"You look for Jason by you own self," he said angrily. "I goin' to meet Buka!"

Seven

My paramount object in this struggle is to save the Union and is not either to save or destroy slavery.

President Abraham Lincoln
August 22, 1862

Rayford led them behind the large oak trees and weeping willows toward the open cotton fields. When they heard growling, Easter grabbed Obi's hand and he spun around. Rayford reached out to a dog that charged from behind one of the trees.

"Hey, boy," he said quietly. "Good boy!" The dog whined contentedly and chewed the small piece of meat Rayford threw to it. Rayford went hunting with George Phillips and knew all of the dogs that were used for plantation patrol.

They made such a winding route through the woods that Obi lost track of the direction in which they travelled. It didn't seem as if they were going toward the Jennings farm and the creek. He wondered who had died and why the funeral was such a big secret. Rayford and the rest of Phillips's people could have obtained real passes to go to a funeral.

There was a constant barking of dogs, and the sound was beginning to unnerve him. Somehow the barks were familiar. Then he realized that they were at the creek near the Jennings farm.

Suddenly a small, hunched figure appeared out of the bushes.

"Buka!" Obi almost yelled. The barking dogs *were* the Jennings's hounds. Easter pulled Obi's arm. "Let's get Jason."

"We have to move on," Buka said. "Them dogs know our smell. Wake the family an' find us like bear trackin' honey."

"Hurry!" Julius whispered to them.

"Obi, please!" Easter grabbed his arm. "We sneak in the house an' get Jason easy."

"I not goin' back there. You go!" he said harshly.

She followed him silently.

After walking for nearly an hour, Obi was startled by the unexpected light of pine torches. A group of mourners walked slowly into a small slave cemetery on the outskirts of a farm. Rayford and Julius fell in step with the mourners, and Obi, Easter, and Buka followed. There were about twenty men and women. Six of the men carried a plain pine box.

Several of the women began to sing a dirge as they approached an open grave. Obi had heard those songs before—so different from their work and play songs.

The other mourners took up the song, and the coffin was placed on the ground next to the grave. When the men pulled up the lid, Obi couldn't believe his eyes. As the light of the torches fell on the contents of the coffin, he saw that it was filled with shotguns, rifles, daggers, and anything else that could be used as a weapon.

While they sang, the mourners reached into their sacks and deposited more weapons. Buka led Obi and Easter behind a tree, away from the light of the torches.

"We runnin' tonight like we planned," Buka rasped. "I got britches for you an' the boy," he said to Easter.

"I can't leave without Jason!" she cried.

"There's no help for it," Obi said sharply.

Buka patted her hand. "No time to go back, daughter. It take a while to get to the farm. We have to be long gone from here by sunup."

"We can't go without him," she repeated. "No one makin' me go." She stood before them with her arms crossed.

"We go east to the swamp," Buka patiently explained. "We return to the farm, then we get caught for sure. Dogs track us to the edge of the land."

"Jason waitin' for us!" she replied with a determined face.

Obi clenched his fists. "Then go back for Jason! Me an' Buka leavin'. I tell you at Master Phillips, we can't get Jason."

"I goin' back." Tears streamed down her face. "He waitin' for us an' we never come. I go with Rayford an' them."

"They won't take you back to the plantation," Buka said. "When Obi discovered missin', you the first one your master come to. They beat the truth out of you."

"I won't tell nothin', an' I ain't afraid of beatin'," Easter said, her firm voice beginning to tremble.

"Can't take that chance, daughter," Buka insisted. He took the overalls and a shirt out of his bulging sack. "Maybe we find Jason when the war done."

"I not goin' without Jason."

Obi was about to grab Easter and shake some sense into her.

"Rayford shoot you before he let you go back. You can't return because you know about all this funeral business now," Buka whispered.

Easter stared at the old man in disbelief, but she accepted the overalls he handed her. Obi and Buka turned their backs while she changed. After she put on the man's shirt and overalls worn by the plantation slaves, Buka gave her a large straw hat. He took her dress and apron and, borrowing a torch from one of the mourners, burned her clothing.

The singing stopped. Obi watched the mourners turn around and walk slowly from the grave containing its coffin of guns. Rayford and Julius walked over to Buka and Obi, and they all embraced. When Rayford rested his hand on Obi's shoulder, Easter watched resentfully.

"God be with all of you," Rayford said as he handed Buka a shotgun. He then joined Julius in the line of mourners. Buka hid the gun in the sack as the torchlight disappeared with the mourners.

"We walk till light, then we hide in the wood," he said.

Obi took the sack from Buka and slipped the pass Rayford had given him inside. As they picked their way through thickets and brambles, Easter walked silently between Obi and Buka.

"We must move fast," Buka warned. "When the overseer know you gone, they use the Jennings dogs to track you. Them hounds know your scent."

Buka right. Them dogs run to us barkin' an' waggin' their tail, Obi said to himself. He wondered how fast or far Buka could walk, but Buka limped along at a surprising speed.

Easter, looking like a slim, young boy, still wasn't speaking.

After walking for a couple of hours, they stopped and rested in a spot thick with vines and underbrush. It was so dark, they could barely see their hands before them. Buka wearily eased his body to the ground and leaned against a log. Obi sat next to him, but Easter kept her distance. She drew up her knees and rested her head on them.

Obi told Buka about Jeremiah's capture. "We might have to use this shotgun on Yankee as well as snake," Buka said, looking at the sack lying at his feet. "Carry the gun," he told Obi, "though I don't think Yankee trouble us. From what you say, seem like Jeremiah went to them, an' that's where he make he mistake—trustin' white mens."

Obi wiped his face on the sleeve of his shirt. The moist, heavy air was filled with the sweetish smell of rotting wood. "How far is we from the Jennings farm?" Obi asked anxiously.

"Not far enough," Buka answered. "But no one lookin' for us yet."

Wiping his face again, Obi sighed. "But Buka, I askin' you how far we is. I know we not far enough."

"Only three mile or so," he answered finally. Shifting his weight and grunting a little, he said, "Now let me tell both of you this plan before we go farther."

Easter didn't change her position or make a sound.

"We goin' to the river. My friend Gabriel, from years gone by when I live on the rice plantation, have a cabin at the river—on he master's farm. He have a boat. He use this boat to carry the sheaves of rice from the island to the rice mill on the mainland side of the river."

"Do he know my mother?" Obi interrupted him.

"Obi, that a long time ago. Even I just know her from the day I see her at the boat. Didn't I tell you that?"

"Yes, Buka," Obi said softly.

"Gabriel take us to the other side of the river, to the island."

"How you know he still there?" Obi asked.

"I just hopin'. I see him a few years ago when I walk this same path we takin' now an' visit he and Mariah, he wife, at the farm."

"What we do if he not there?"

"We get across. The farm belong to Master Turner. Master Turner and he family only stay at the big house by the river in the summer. The rest of the time they on the island, an' just the overseer an' some of the slaves run the farm."

"But it summer now. Suppose the master still there?"

"It almost August. I remember Gabriel tell me Master an' Mistress leave the highland farm, as they call it, by the end of July, when the rice field drain. We mix in with the slaves. Don't worry. We get far as the river. Somebody take us across in the boat."

Buka started to cough then, and Obi patted him on his back. The old man cleared his throat. "I okay. Now, listen,

Easter name is Ezra if we caught. Obi, you an' Ezra is my two grandson. The patteroller do what they want with her if they find she a girl."

Easter still sat quietly with her head on her knees. "Remember, Easter, your name Ezra now, an' you an' Obi my grandson," he repeated. She didn't respond.

"You hear what Buka tellin' you, Easter. You answer!" Obi said angrily.

She raised her head. "My name Ezra," she said dully.

"Now, the next thing is this," Buka continued. "I not able to get to Rayford soon enough for he to make us a pass like I plan. So we have to say we lose we pass if patteroller stop us," Buka chuckled. "I yell an' make fuss with you, Obi. Like you the one lose it."

"But we have pass, Buka!" Obi pulled Buka's arm excitedly. Then he related the story of how Rayford had helped him.

"That pass most likely for Brantley's farm, Obi. None of us can read, so we don't know what it say." He thought a while. "Maybe the pass help us if we stopped. I have to think on it, Obi. It dangerous to show pass an' not know what it say."

Buka eased himself off the ground slowly. "We best move on. Have a long way to go."

Obi picked up the sack and placed the shotgun over his shoulder. Easter stood up, her face hidden by the big straw hat and the dark night.

As they started to walk, Obi asked Buka another question: "Why Rayford and them sneakin' guns in coffins?"

"They storin' guns in case the white men stop fightin' each other and fight blacks. An' they helpin' runaways like us. See, one of them women at the funeral bring me clothes an' the food we need. The huntin' knife is mine, though," he added.

They continued walking until they could go no farther. Even Obi was beginning to stumble from exhaustion, and Buka coughed frequently.

Easter still hadn't said anything. They crawled into a thicket of leaves and vines just as the birds were beginning to sing. Soon all three were asleep.

At first Obi didn't remember where he was when he woke up. Easter slept against his shoulder, and Buka snored heavily on Obi's other side. Carefully, he placed Easter's head on the leaf-covered ground and crawled out of their enclosure. Easter stirred and moaned slightly. Rays of light filtered through the tall oaks, cypresses, and other trees. A rabbit scampered under a bush and startled him.

He opened the sack and took out a potato and a piece of bread. Rummaging inside the sack again, he found a package of dried, salted beef. He put it back, so that they could have it to eat in the evening. While he ate his breakfast, Easter crawled out of the thicket.

"Mornin'," Obi said, handing her a potato. She ignored him, got her own food out of the sack, and ate in silence.

Obi was unable to stand her stubbornness any longer.

"We couldn't help it, Easter. We had to leave Jason."

She stared at him mutely.

"*You* say you want to run. *You* say you want us to be together," he said accusingly, picking up a small stone.

"*Us* mean Jason too," she said.

He threw the stone into a clump of bushes. "I have to find my ma! Jason be fine. They not sellin' him in the Charleston market like me."

She turned her back on him and lay down to rest again. She did not say another word to him. While Obi finished eating, Buka left the shelter. Obi watched anxiously as Buka tried to control his hacking cough. When he stopped coughing, Obi handed him a potato.

"This a good spot to hide," Buka said, looking around at the dense growth of trees and brush.

For the rest of the day, they slept on and off until nightfall.

Before they continued their journey, Buka took Obi aside

and cautioned him. "Watch Easter. She mind might tell she to go to Jason."

"She don't know these woods. Get lost if she leave us," Obi said.

"The dumbest woman be smarter than man, remember that, Obi."

Once again they walked all night, covering more miles than they did the night before. Obi watched Easter carefully, though he didn't think she would try to leave them. He was more worried about Buka's coughing and the faint sounds of barking dogs.

"It have a lot of hunters in the swamp. That be their hounds," Buka told him. They trekked through the woods until the ground began to soften under their feet. "We nearin' the swamp now," Buka said and paused. "We walk till the light come up." He started to walk again and stumbled.

Obi reached for him. "Let me carry you, Buka," he offered.

Buka shooed him away. "I fine. We stop soon an' find shelter." They continued walking until the ground became muddy. They stepped carefully, making sure that what looked like a tree branch in the dark was not really a snake.

As the sky began to lighten, they reached an area of firmer ground covered with tall grass. They decided to stop and sleep. Obi wished he knew what Easter was thinking as she helped him gather branches and leaves for them to crawl under.

Easter took shelter first. "Keep watch a while," Buka whispered to Obi. "Make sure it safe here." Obi sat down, holding the shotgun across his knees. He thought about Wilson and John Jennings and wondered how far they'd tracked them and in what direction they'd gone.

Obi couldn't keep watch very long and soon fell asleep from exhaustion. When he woke up, he immediately reached for the shotgun and checked to see whether Easter was still in the shelter. She slept soundly next to Buka.

He stood up stiffly and looked around. Though sunlight

had ·brightened the swamp somewhat, shadow and mist seemed to be there permanently. Greyish-brown moss hung heavily from the large oak trees. These, along with high grasses, created a natural shelter.

Obi listened carefully for the dreaded sound of dogs and spun around when he heard a slight rustling near him. Easter crawled out of the shelter. She opened the sack and took out a potato, acting as if Obi wasn't there.

"Easter, you tell me you want to run," he said, pointing his finger in her face as she leaned over the sack. "I tell you it best you stay, but your head hard as stone." Easter sat down, took a bite out of the potato, and stared at a lizard as it slithered over a log. Obi gave up. He walked over to a little brook a few feet away. Dousing his face with the cool, clear water, he decided not to worry about Easter anymore.

She head too thick to understand why we have to leave Jason.

Buka crept slowly and painfully from under the pile of leaves. He barely nibbled at a piece of meat while Obi and Easter prepared to start out. "Children, you keep walking east," he said slowly. "The way the sun rise. Remember, when you get to the river, you see the farm. Gabriel take you 'cross the river in the boat. Remember he name— Gabriel."

Obi peered into Buka's creased, black face. "You talk like you not goin'," he said anxiously.

"Who know what happen in this life, Obi," Buka mumbled. "You get there. I see to that."

Obi looked at Easter. She had turned her face away from them.

By the third night of running, their bodies seemed to melt into the shadows and take the shape of the trees and bushes. Buka "saw" with his ears, hands, and feet as well as his eyes. Once he limped into a spot and immediately backed away. "Quicksand," he had said, feeling the ground with his hands and practically crawling. "Walk here—this firmer ground."

Obi noticed that Buka had slowed his pace quite a bit

after they had walked a while. "I carry you," Obi said. This time Buka accepted his offer.

He lifted the old man onto his back, and Easter picked up the sack and the gun. "Step careful," he rasped into Obi's ear. "Put one foot before the other. You feel sinkin', then you stop. We goin' through thick mud an' then a creek. After that the ground firm up. When you feel it firm, you near the farm."

"You goin' there with us. Why you waste breath for so much direction?" Obi tried to sound confident, but he was nervous. He listened to the barking, which had started up again.

"You have to know what to do," Buka said. He began to cough and choke. Obi put him down until the old man caught his breath. Easter stood silently, still holding the sack and gun, watching while Obi patted Buka on his back. When Buka's cough quieted, Obi noticed that another sound had also ceased—there were no more sounds from the dogs. He didn't know whether to feel relieved or whether the silence was an ill omen.

"Another two hour—if you walk fast—you reach the river. Nobody lookin' for me. I slowin' you down. Leave me here."

"I ain't leavin' you, Buka," Obi said firmly.

"Yes—I meet you on the other side. I know the way, Obi."

"No, I ain't leavin' you," Obi insisted. "You stay, then I stayin' too." Obi bent down so that Buka could climb on his back. The old man got on hesitantly.

They moved on again, but Buka's breathing was heavy and labored. Soon they were sloshing through thick mud. *Least we gettin' near now, an' no one find us yet,* Obi told himself.

Easter, the sack slung over her shoulder and the shotgun cradled in her arm, stumbled a few times but kept her balance. Besides the clothing intended for Jason, the only articles remaining in the sack were a few slices of bread, the pass, and Buka's hunting knife.

After walking a while longer, they came to the creek. *We almost at the river an' the island!* Obi realized. He was afraid to get excited about being so close to what he'd always dreamed about—afraid he would wake up in the hayloft at the Jennings farm and find that he'd only been dreaming.

The creek water felt cool and refreshing around his long legs after wading through so much mud. Obi wished he could take off his clothes and wash. Though he'd vowed to ignore Easter, he spoke to her as they crossed the creek.

"Be careful, the rocks slippery."

No sooner had the words left his mouth than she slipped and fell in the water. Obi, reaching for her, almost lost balance himself. Buka held onto Obi's shoulders. "Lawd," he mumbled. "Should a use me own foot for this trip." Obi managed to steady himself.

"My foot surer than yours," Obi teased him.

"Thank you, Obi," Easter murmured as she took Obi's outstretched hand. On her feet again, she pulled the straw hat, the sack, and the gun out of the water.

"You welcome," Obi said, surprised that she had spoken, let alone thanked him. Easter shook the water out of the hat, and they completed their crossing. He couldn't bear to look at the water rolling off the gun. *That gun can't shoot nothin' now.*

"Put me down," Buka demanded as soon as they got to the other side. He cleared his throat. "I can walk some."

Easter was soaked from head to foot and tried to wring out the water from the legs of her overalls. Obi did the same, but it was hard to wring out clothes while still wearing them.

He looked at Buka and smiled. "See, you the only one who dry, an' you complainin'."

"An' I the only one who almost die in that creek," Buka joked. They trudged along until the trees stood farther apart and the bushes and shrubs thinned out. A chink of light in the east indicated sunrise, but there were still enough trees and predawn darkness to hide them.

After a while, Buka stopped. "We rest here," he breathed

heavily. "Only for a bit. We almost to the river." He sat down wearily under the dangling branches of a willow. Easter and Obi joined him. The delicate leaves hung like tassels over them. The nearest tree, about fifteen feet away, was a cypress, its roots protruding from the ground.

Easter opened the sack and removed some soggy bread.

"Don't think the birds even want that," Buka told her when she threw the bread in a clump of bushes. He turned to Obi. "Put the gun in the sack. You gonna have to clean that good, else it won't work again. Water ruin it."

Obi rested his head against the tree and looked up at a piece of sky, painted mauve by the rising sun. Then he sat up quickly and slapped his forehead. "Buka, that pass. It probably ruin like the bread! Now we—" He didn't have time to complete his sentence. Just beyond the cypress, a group of white men carrying rifles was headed toward them.

Eight

When de War begin dey carried Young Marster off . . . and
dey sent me to wait on him. . . . Colonel Farrabow . . .
told us to go to the breastworks and work.

George Rogers, ex-slave
From *Voices from Slavery*

Easter let go of the sack, and Obi stared while Buka rose
stiffly from the ground. A man with a long, thick, hay-
colored beard and a slouch hat like the one Wilson wore
approached them.

Three others, one of them black, followed. Obi's heart
raced as Buka steadied himself, placing his gnarled hand
on the tree.

"Caught us some big rabbits, boys," the man with the
beard said, grinning.

"Never know what you might catch in these woods,
Corporal," a tall, skinny man replied. He wore a straw hat
with a wide brim.

Obi stood up, drawing closer to Buka.

"Bet they runaways, Corporal Jameson," said a youthful
looking fellow. He had pale blue eyes and thick yellow hair.
"We give 'em back to their owners, maybe get some money
for 'em."

Except for the black man, the rest of them laughed at

the yellow-haired boy. "Don't be stupid, Simon," Corporal Jameson said. "We got a war to fight."

The black man said nothing. He was tall, with a large frame and a round, tan-colored face. He wore overalls, a straw hat, and carried two croaker sacks and a rifle. One of the sacks bulged as if it contained a couple of rabbits.

"We not runaways, suh." Buka spoke calmly to Jameson, who seemed to be the leader of the group.

"What you doin' in these woods, then, old man? Huntin'?"

Obi glanced at Easter, who kept her head lowered. He felt like a little bird he'd seen once, flapping its useless wings against a raging storm.

Obi guessed that they were soldiers because they called the bearded one Corporal, but he wasn't sure. These men, with their light-brown trousers, shirts, and different hats, were sloppily dressed.

Then he noticed that the young boy named Simon wore a soft, grey cap. He recognized it—maybe they *were* Confederate soldiers. Buka, like an actor, changed his tone of voice. "Suh, we ain't no runaways," he said humbly, addressing Corporal Jameson again.

"We let the Colonel figure out whether you runaways or not," Corporal Jameson said. He pushed Easter in front of him. "Boy, you walk ahead of me," he ordered.

Least the disguise workin', Obi thought.

"Smith," Jameson said to the skinny man, "you get behind that tall one." He pointed to Obi.

Obi studied the black man who walked next to Smith. For a moment, Obi thought the man looked at him with sympathy.

Jameson moved Easter quickly along. Obi reached down and quickly picked up the sack that Easter had left.

"Gimme that," Smith demanded.

Snatching the sack from Obi, Smith pulled out the shotgun. "We better show this to the Colonel," he said to Simon.

Simon pushed Buka ahead of him and Buka stumbled. Obi winced when Simon poked Buka in his back with his rifle. Without thinking, he pushed the soldier aside and clasped his hand around Buka's arm. "He old. He can't move fast," he said angrily.

Simon stared at Obi in surprise, and Smith aimed his rifle at Obi's head. "Boy, you're in trouble now. I should shoot you for that!"

Obi's large eyes seemed to sink deeper inside his head as he stared at Smith.

"The boy grab for he grandfather—he push Simon by accident," the black man said, grinning at Smith.

"You sure about that, Daniel?"

"Yes, suh." Daniel kept his round face grinning.

"Suh," Buka said, "the boy know I sick and he afraid I get hurt."

"Old man, you live this long 'cause you had sense enough not to fight no white man." Smith stepped close to Obi, who could smell the scent of tobacco in the man's rumpled shirt. "Don't have no more accidents, hear?"

"Yes, suh," Obi said softly. *Long as that farm boy don't have no more accident with he rifle.* "Can I carry my grandfather, suh?"

"Suit yourself, but let's git."

Obi lifted Buka and carried him as before. They reached a clearing where trees had recently been felled and freshly cut logs lay on the ground. There were no people about, but Obi thought he heard voices in the distance, though it was hard to tell with Daniel and the soldiers laughing and talking.

As they continued walking, Obi heard a man shout, and he also thought he smelled bacon and coffee. Then they came to a field covered with sturdy-looking tents. Soldiers were lining up for breakfast. A black man, standing over a large, three-legged iron skillet, served coffee, bacon, and grits.

"I walk now," Buka rasped in Obi's ear as they picked

their way among the tents. Obi put him down. "Look there," Buka said, pointing straight ahead. "The Edisto River. This the farm."

The river looked like a silver ribbon in the distance. Obi gave Buka a puzzled look as Jameson hurried them through the camp.

How could this be a farm, he wondered, *with so many soldiers?*

Obi looked to his left and saw tall, green stalks of corn. Peas, okra, collards, and other crops grew in several nearby fields. Cows and horses could be seen grazing in pastures beyond the fields.

To his right, he saw a row of small stick-and-mud shacks and some tents put together with old canvas and stakes. Daniel tossed the sacks and rifle to Smith. "Save some of that rabbit for me," he said and walked in the direction of the broken-down shacks.

When they neared the riverbank, Obi saw the gun barrels mounted on two-wheeled carriages, the ammunition chests, and the soldiers manning the weapons. A long ditch, looking like a scar in the ground, had been dug a few feet behind the artillery. The sun was now positioned over the horizon.

They stopped in front of a large, white, two-story frame house with a spacious porch. Smith handed Buka's sack to Corporal Jameson.

"They carryin' weapons," he said.

"Go get the Colonel," Jameson ordered. Smith ran up the steps and knocked on the door. Obi was feeling so weary he could have stretched under the hedges that circled the building and gone fast asleep. Buka, standing next to Obi, looked as if he were about to collapse. Easter kept her head lowered.

Obi could see a mass of land—the island—on the other side of the river. It was so close! The colonel came out of the house. His dark-brown mustache reminded Obi of the captain who'd come to the Jennings farm. He motioned to Jameson to bring them up on the porch.

"Y'all can leave now," Jameson said to Smith and Simon. They took off in the direction of the tents.

"What's this, Jameson?" the colonel asked with a bored and disgusted expression. He wore a grey tunic jacket and looked the way Obi thought a soldier was supposed to look.

Obi tried to read the man's heavily lidded, brown eyes in order to discover just what kind of person the colonel might be.

"Found them in the woods, sir. Say they ain't runaways, but I don't believe them."

"You all runaways?" Colonel Andrews asked.

"No, suh," Buka said.

"We took this off them, Colonel Andrews," Jameson interrupted, holding up the shotgun. He handed it to Andrews.

The colonel inspected the gun. "Give it to the quartermaster."

Colonel Andrews stared at the three of them again. "I believe you are runaways. Now, don't make me beat the truth out of you."

"Probably stole the gun too," Jameson said.

"Suh, there's a pass in the sack," Buka said calmly. "We ain't no runaways."

Jameson rummaged through the sack and pulled out the damp piece of paper.

"That's we pass," Buka said hoarsely and then began to cough.

Jameson handed Colonel Andrews the paper. "I can't read this—it's all smeared," Andrews said. Obi was relieved.

Jameson continued rummaging through the sack. "Look what else is here—a huntin' knife and some trousers."

Colonel Andrews looked up from the paper he'd been turning from front to back. "Maybe this was a pass, but it seems to me that you wouldn't just drop something as important as a pass in an old croaker sack. Where were you going?"

" 'Cross the river to the island, suh. I born there and want my grandsons to take me back."

Andrews put his hands in his pockets. A slight smile played around his mouth. "Old man, you've been lying longer than I've been living." He looked at the paper again. "This is worthless," he said, crushing the paper. "I think you're trying to reach those Union gunboats on the ocean.

"Old man," he continued, "you can go back to wherever it is you came from." He looked at Jameson. "Put the two boys with the other slaves. They look healthy enough. We can use them for the trenches." Then he took a second glance at Easter, who still held her head down. "Put him in the field."

"And Jameson," the colonel added, "you hear about people's slaves running off the farms around here, let me know. We'll return these when we finish with the trenches and breastworks. Nobody's going across that river." He walked toward the door of the house.

Obi shot a quick glance across the water to the island. It seemed as if he could stretch out his arm and touch it.

Easter raised her head. "I can cook, suh," she said softly.

Obi clenched his fists. *She don't care who she slave for, long as she ain't in no field.*

"I won't stand for somebody messing up my food. Can you really cook, boy?"

"Yes, suh," she said firmly.

The colonel didn't seem to take any more notice of Easter. He put his hand on the doorknob. "Jameson, give the two boys something to eat. They've got a busy day ahead of them."

Jameson led them in the direction of the shacks they'd just passed. He gave the sack to Buka after removing the hunting knife. Easter walked alongside Jameson.

They reached a shed where a man and a woman prepared breakfast for the camp. Black men in overalls were coming out of the nearby tents and shacks, headed for the cooking shed. The man and woman were old, but not as old as

Buka. She was short and wiry and had her head wrapped in a clean, white cloth. The man was also slight.

The woman took the lid off the skillet and stirred the grits as steam rose out of the pot. "Feed these two boys," Jameson told the woman. "The old man gets nothin'. You hear me? Nothin'."

She nodded, staring at Buka closely.

Jameson turned to the grey-haired man, who was putting tin plates on a table. "Take the small one to the field with you this mornin'," he said, pointing to Easter.

"Yes, suh," the man answered pleasantly, staring at Buka as if he had never seen him before. The men were beginning to line up in front of the shed. "Get on line," Jameson ordered Obi and Easter. "I'll be back for you," he told Obi and headed quickly toward the soldiers' tents at the other end of the farm.

The woman handed her large, wooden spoon to one of the men on line and rushed to Buka. The grey-haired man followed. "Lord, is it you, Buka?" She grabbed him around his shoulders.

Buka nodded. "It's me, an' my two grandson," he said, winking.

"Obi, Ezra, this Mariah an' Gabriel."

"Welcome," the woman said.

"They runnin'?" Gabriel whispered.

"Yes. I takin' them to the island—to Green Hills Plantation."

"You come bad time," Mariah said. Her husband nodded in agreement.

"The soldiers take over the farm since this war business. Old Master die three year ago, an' he son take over," she continued. Her small, black eyes slanted over her high, sharp cheekbones. "He give this farm to the Confederates." Her eyes darted back and forth as if someone were watching her.

"The soldiers stretch the big gun along the river. Say Yankees try to get to Charleston from here." She moved her long, thin fingers as she talked. "Master and Mistress stay on the island. Me, Gabriel, an' some of the hands from the plantation told to stay here an' grow food for the soldiers."

"They have slave from other plantations too," Gabriel said. "They buildin' wall an' diggin' big, big ditch they call trench." He spread his arms to demonstrate how wide and long the trenches were.

Obi noticed that the men were now sitting on the ground eating their breakfast of grits. They didn't have bacon and coffee like the white soldiers. A few of them ate with wooden spoons, but most scooped up the grits with clam shells.

"I don't care what that Jameson say," Mariah said to Buka as she touched his arm, "I feedin' you."

"We give him some of our food," Obi offered. "Don't want these soldier to trouble you."

"I ain't scare of no soldier. Buka like family. I take he to our cabin, an' he stay with us long as he want to." She patted Buka on his back but looked at Obi. "You an' your brother stay with us too," she said.

Buka seemed as if he were going to faint. "No food now, Mariah, just rest. Then I tell you the whole story." His voice faded into a dry cough.

Gabriel turned to Mariah. "I finish servin' the men. You take Buka to the cabin."

After they got their grits, Easter and Obi sat outside the shed under an oak tree. Easter rested her plate on the ground and covered her face.

"Why you tell that man you a cook?" Obi asked her. "You think we stayin' here?"

She uncovered her face and looked at him. "I not a field hand. I a cook, an' I ain't stayin' here neither 'cause they be sendin' us back—an' I glad!" she said, almost in tears. "I don't want to be under that burnin' sun in the field." She turned her back on him and scooped up some of the grits in the shell, twisting her mouth in disgust as she put the shell to her lips.

Easter ate a bit more in silence. Then she stuck the shell into the food and put the plate on the ground. "Soldier have you an' me now, Obi. An' Jason still waitin' for us."

"I tell you to stay," he said, loud enough for some to hear him.

"Where you from?" a familiar voice called out. "Who your master?" Obi hadn't seen Daniel sit down with a group of men under a nearby tree.

"Ain't got none," Obi mumbled, his eyes avoiding Daniel's. He was too upset to talk to a stranger—even one who had helped him.

"You free?" Daniel asked, finishing off his food.

Obi ignored the question and looked away. Daniel, shrugging his shoulders, got up and headed to the cooking shed.

Obi noticed Jameson strolling in their direction. When he reached them, the corporal threw a pair of mustard-colored trousers and a white shirt at Easter.

"The Colonel needs a servant boy. Clean your whole self. There's a water pump back of them shacks. Can't go smellin' up the Colonel's house. When you finish, go there. He waitin' for you." He turned to Obi. "I'll be back for you."

Obi thought that Jameson's eyes looked a little glazed, as if he'd been drinking.

He left and Obi squeezed Easter's arm. "I told you! You should keep your mouth shut about cookin'."

She pulled away. "I a cook."

"How you gonna wash in the pump an' you supposed to be a boy?"

"I manage."

Mariah, back from the cabin, walked over to them. "Buka restin'," she said, looking at Easter. "He tell me you posin' as a boy. It a good idea, especially in this camp with all these men. It okay for a old woman like me but not for a pretty girl."

"Everybody know her secret soon!" Obi said angrily. He explained to Mariah what had just happened.

To his surprise, the old woman smiled. "Good! She don't need to be in the field. This way I don't have to be troublin' myself cookin' for the Colonel. I got all these men to cook for."

"Where she gonna wash?" Obi asked her.

"I take care of that. She bathe back of my cabin. Nobody see her." She tried to peer under Easter's straw hat. "You have a lot of hair?"

Easter nodded.

"I cut that. Make you look like a real boy."

Easter left with Mariah and Obi looked around him. Some of the men had finished eating and gone to the field, while Daniel and a few of the others were on their way to the riverbank. Another group, carrying axes and saws, headed for the clearing in the woods. Others cleaned around the tents of the white soldiers and the rest of the campgrounds.

The air was becoming humid. Obi stood up as Jameson approached. He followed the man toward the riverbank. Glancing in the direction of the tents, Obi saw lines of soldiers standing before other soldiers who called out names.

"Never seen nothin' like this, have you, boy?" Jameson sneered as they walked. They were nearing the black men digging the trenches.

"Let me tell you somethin'," he said, turning to face Obi. He pointed to the river. "See, over that way is east, headin' to the Atlantic Ocean." Then he pointed to the colonel's house. "That way is south—takes you down through Georgia and Florida—and soldiers there too."

He spread his arms to indicate the woods that surrounded the farm like a horseshoe. "There is soldiers all through them woods. I don't know how y'all didn't get caught before we found you."

Obi wondered what Jameson was trying to say.

"What I'm tellin' you is this:"—he leaned close to Obi—"you belong to us now, and you can't get away."

Nine

In South Carolina, black folk floated to freedom on "basket boats made out of reeds," thus reviving an ancient African craft.

Vincent Harding, author
From *There Is a River*

September 1861

Obi had fallen uncomfortably into the routine of the camp. He and the other slaves had finished the trenches and were now building protective walls for the gunners at the river-bank.

"They bringin' in new soldier all the time. Gettin' ready for a real fight maybe," Daniel said.

Obi was startled. He hadn't noticed Daniel standing beside him as he hammered in a plank of wood.

"Maybe," Obi mumbled. Rumors about Yankees and up-coming battles drifted through the camp like the river mists. He paid little mind to them.

Daniel looked around the riverbank. "Guess Jameson settin' with he whiskey jug." He rested his elbow on one of the planks and watched the soldiers. "If they's a battle, these soldier be busy. Too busy to worry with us."

Obi nodded and continued working. He'd said little to Daniel or any of the other men in the camp since he'd been there. He was only interested in Buka's getting well so that they could get on with their journey.

On clear days like this one, when the sun burned away the fog and mist, he could see the island, just within reach— yet almost impossible to get to.

"These soldiers start fightin' them Yankees, that be the perfect time to run," Daniel muttered. He stared at Obi as if measuring the effect of his words.

Obi was interested, but he wasn't going to be baited. "You don't like it here?" he asked, hammering in another piece of wood.

"Like it much as you do," Daniel said. His voice was serious. "I have a woman an' child on the island. I miss them." He was from the same plantation as Mariah and Gabriel.

Obi had never seen the serious side of the man, who always seemed to be laughing and joking with the other slaves and the soldiers. His face looked different without the smile—older and harder.

Picking up another plank, Obi said, "So when the war done, you go back."

"That might take too long."

A man working near Daniel nudged him. "There go that Ezra, the Colonel's boy, gatherin' palm leaf an' reed with he own little hands."

Obi looked up from his work and saw Easter strolling along the riverbank with an armload of grasses and palm fronds. Her short-cropped hair made her small face and smiling, brown eyes stand out even more. He hated hearing the men ridicule her. "He just a young boy," Obi snapped.

"I just teasin' about your little brother," the man said and went back to work.

Obi didn't answer but banged the nail so hard that the wood splintered. Daniel watched him for a moment. "You love your brother. When we know we family we best love 'em," he muttered, watching Obi closely.

Obi sensed that Daniel might suspect that Ezra was a

girl. Since he was friendly with Mariah and Gabriel, he was often in the cabin when Easter was there.

Most of the time Easter was cooking, cleaning, and washing for Colonel Andrews. Sometimes, though, she would sit in the cabin in the evening. Mariah was teaching her how to make baskets and rugs out of the palm fronds and grasses.

The conch horn blew to signal lunch, and Obi walked alone to the cooking shed. Mariah was dishing out the food. He picked up a plate from the pine table and walked over to her.

"Obi," she said, nervously spooning the food onto his plate, "when you go in to see Buka, try and make he eat."

Obi had been eating his lunch each day in the cabin with Buka. Buka ate little, usually drinking something Mariah made from molasses, vinegar, and water. He rarely left the cabin. Sometimes in the evening, when the heat inside was unbearable, he'd sit on the porch with Obi.

A few others, including Daniel, would occasionally join them and talk to Buka.

"He not eatin' at all?" Obi asked Mariah.

"No, not even he grits in the mornin'. Maybe he eat some of this," she said, placing an extra spoonful of peas and rice on Obi's plate.

Obi walked quickly to the cabin. Buka, lying on a straw mattress near the entrance, smiled weakly as Obi helped him sit up. He was glad that Buka was awake. Some days he slept the whole time Obi was there. "How you today, Obi?"

"I fine." Obi sat cross-legged in front of him on a mat that Mariah had woven to cover the dirt floor. "Buka, Mariah tell me you ain't been eatin'." He rested his plate on the floor and, taking a spoonful of rice, put it up to Buka's lips. "Here, let me feed you this."

Buka lay back down and shook his head. "No. I don't eat noon meal."

"You don't eat *no* meal. Come outside and sit. Take some air."

He closed his eyes. "Tomorrow—I sit out tomorrow."

"You need to eat. You get your strength and we cross the river."

"Not hungry," he said.

"We have to go to the island. You help me find Lorena."

"I goin' pass that river and pass that island." He turned slowly on his side and watched Obi. "Lorena was a long time ago. You have to move on."

Obi didn't understand. "I know, then you an' me an' Easter, we go on to Mexico."

Buka patted Obi's knee with his wrinkled hand. "You born a man, not a slave—that the thing to remember. You got to learn which way freedom be. It here first," he said, touching his own creased forehead. "In you own mind."

Obi stared blankly at his old friend.

"This a time for joy. The ancestors call me an' I go see them. Think hard an' you find a way to get to the island. My time done." He closed his eyes.

Obi touched Buka's feverish forehead gently. "Buka, how I find a way without you?"

Buka opened his eyes slowly—like the sun fighting to rise over thick clouds. "You find a way," he said, gazing at the top of Obi's bent head.

"You know, my real name *Baako*. It mean 'firstborn.' Over the years people say the name wrong, so I known as Buka now. You as much my firstborn as if you was made from my flesh. You know which way freedom be now. You leave one master—you find a way to leave this soldier master too."

Obi nodded, not able to speak. Buka coughed and when he caught his breath, Obi could barely hear him.

"Let me rest."

Buka closed his eyes for the last time, and Obi watched the life seep out of him. He was still staring at Buka when Daniel rushed into the cabin.

"Jameson lookin' for you!"

Obi knocked over the plate of food as he jumped to his feet. Daniel started to say something else but stopped short when he saw Buka lying on the floor. He peered closely at the old man and then bent down and took Buka's wrist. "He dead," he whispered. "I get the boys to come bury him."

"He have to get a right burial," Obi told him. "I makin' a coffin an' he be bury proper."

"You crazy? You think these soldier let you use they wood an' time to make a coffin?"

Pushing Daniel aside, Obi left the cabin. No one—not even the colonel himself—was going to stop him from making Buka's coffin.

He went to the shed, where Mariah was washing plates in a large tin tub. "Buka dead," he announced.

Mariah looked at Obi calmly. "I prepare the body," she said.

Obi ran to the clearing where several of the black laborers were stacking wood. Daniel dashed behind him, breathing heavily.

"Obi, Jameson gettin' angry."

Ignoring him, Obi pulled out a piece of wood large enough for one of the sides of the coffin. "I makin' Buka's coffin."

"Wait till tonight," Daniel said, "an' I help you."

"Can't wait," Obi answered and continued to search for more wood.

"Then I start makin' the coffin for you. Jameson ain't gonna say nothin' to me. I tell he I makin' a trap for huntin'. You go back so he see you there workin'. When he leave, then you come back here an' finish the coffin."

"Thank you, Daniel," Obi said quietly and returned to the breastworks at the riverbank.

They buried Buka that night under a cypress tree where the woods behind the slave cabins began. Mariah and Gabriel quietly sang a wailing, high-pitched funeral dirge that reminded Obi of the mock funeral they'd attended only a few months ago. The single pine torch cast a dim light on their small circle.

Besides Daniel, some of the other blacks in the camp were there to pay their last respects to the old African. They were those who sat in front of Mariah and Gabriel's shack sometimes.

When the grave was covered over, Mariah said the Twenty-third Psalm while Easter placed a cross she'd woven out of the dried grass on the mound of dirt to mark the gravesite. Obi wiped his eyes on his shirtsleeves as he thought about Buka and him fishing together and hunting small game.

They trudged back to the cabin. Easter walked next to Obi. "Why you didn't tell me that he dead?" she asked. "Daniel have to bring the news."

"I didn't think you care about Buka dyin'. Didn't think you was comin' to he funeral."

"Why? He suppose to be my grandfather too!" she said angrily. "I not mad at he. The old man die helpin' us. He know he too old an' sick to make this trip to the river. But he come anyway. For us—for you."

She paused a moment. "It's you, Obi. You act like you care for nothin' but you self. Even if you try a little to go back for Jason, you act like you care nothin' about he."

Obi was glad that the night hid the shame in his eyes. "Easter," Obi whispered, "I promise you we find Jason, and all three of us be together again. I see to that."

A few days after Buka's burial, Obi, Daniel, and the others still worked on the wall. Daniel turned his gaze away from the river and watched a group of slaves carrying shovels, going into the woods.

"These soldier busy, Obi. We go dig pit in the wood. I hear Jameson say the Yankee tryin' to get to Charleston and gonna come through here to do it." He leaned close to Obi. "The first Yankee I see, I runnin' to them. I have to go back to the island."

"Don't think you better run to no Yankee," Obi said. He told him about Jeremiah.

When Obi finished, Daniel picked up his hammer. "I

been hearin' different story, Obi. Slave been runnin' to the Yankee camps like thunder follow lightnin'.'"

"I want to get 'cross that river too," Obi whispered. Then he told Daniel about his dream of finding his mother. "An' after I find her we goin' to Mexico."

"What about your brother?" Daniel asked. "He goin' with you?" He studied Obi with a knowing look in his eyes.

"Yes, he goin' too," Obi mumbled, avoiding Daniel's eyes. He went back to work.

Daniel cleared his throat. "Your brother ain't really your brother, is he? Ezra a girl."

Obi nodded and stared at Daniel. "Don't tell no one."

"I won't. Some of these men an' soldiers trouble her if they know." He smiled. "I suspect for a long time. Don't worry. I watch out for she too."

That evening, as Obi, Gabriel, Mariah, and Daniel sat in the cabin, Obi felt as if Buka were still there with them.

"I bring your pallet inside tonight, Obi. You sleep in here with me an' Gabriel," Mariah said.

"It be gettin' cold, you know, Obi," Gabriel added. "When them rain come an' the storm blow in from the ocean, you can't sleep outside."

"Seven of us piled into that shack I in, an' it still be cold. Have to get some clay an' fill in them cracks," Daniel said.

The cabin door opened and Easter walked in. "What you cook for the Colonel tonight?" Daniel asked. "Bring us anything?"

Easter placed a neatly wrapped package of corn bread and slices of ham on the table. "Keep that hole in your face shut, Daniel. Can't talk whiles you eat," she smiled.

Obi reached for the package first. "Don't tell he that. Think the whole thing for him."

"Next time we catch some rabbit, Easter, I bring one for you to cook. You 'bout the best cook—beside Mariah an' my Minna—that I come 'cross in a long time." Daniel grinned and bit into a piece of ham.

"You just like to keep you belly full," Mariah grumbled.

"You ain't learn yet that slave never get enough to eat."

Easter knelt down at the fire and warmed herself, rubbing her hands together. Then she picked up several blades of dried grass that Mariah had spread out to one side of the fireplace. She took a palmetto frond and started coiling it around the blades of grass.

Mariah had been teaching her how to coil the leaves and grasses, and she was about to make her first basket. Obi left the table and sat next to her so he could watch. "Don't tell me you weavin' basket too, Obi?" Daniel chuckled.

"No," Obi said seriously. "I go weave me a boat."

Ten

*After old Ned got such a terrible beatin' for
prayin' for freedom, he slipped off and went to
de North to join de Union Army.*

Mingo White, ex-slave
From *Voices from Slavery*

October 1861

Everyone except Gabriel stared at him as if he were crazy.
Mariah spoke first. "There a kind of root to make a tea to
calm mad people. I lookin' for some of that root for you
tomorrow, Obi."

Obi stood up. "Gabriel, what you think the length an'
width should be to hold four or five people?"

"Don't put me an' Gabriel in them numbers," Mariah
said as she joined Easter by the fire.

Daniel, laughing, stretched across the bench. "Lord have
mercy. We goin' to ride a basket to freedom."

Gabriel thought a moment. "You could make a boat out
of the grasses. Make one the length an' breadth of a big
cabin—not a shack like this. Like so—" He strode from
the fireplace to the door. "Twelve paces." Then he pointed
from the bed to the other side of the room. "Now if this
shack stretch about eight more steps, that give twenty
paces. That be just right for a boat to get you 'cross the

river. If you want to go 'cross the ocean, now that a different thing."

Mariah peered up at her husband. "You as fool as the boy is," she said.

"My father a African man. He tell me about boats made from reeds," Gabriel said.

Daniel got off the bench and fingered the rug on the floor. "You know, this be strong."

Obi turned to Daniel. "We make it in the cove where the grass tall," he said.

Daniel touched the rug again. "The cove a good place to hide it too. No one go there. We hide it in the grass."

"Then," Obi mused, "when we finish, we take it to that inlet that lead to the river."

"How you sailin' 'cross that river with them gun pointin' at you?" Mariah asked. "They only allow the boats carryin' the rice sheaves and the Confederate ships on the river."

"We leave at night," Obi told her. He was watching Easter make her basket.

Easter looked up from her work. "I hear the Colonel tell he aide that they expect a fight. Say the Yankee go try an' take the island. Then they take over this side an' head for Charleston."

"This boat thing a stupid idea." Mariah sucked her teeth. "So when the Yankee an' the slavers fight, the three of you gonna be in the middle of the river?"

Obi stood up. "I been hearin' about Yankee attack since I been here," he said. "Gabriel, how long it take to make the boat?"

"About a month."

"I ain't goin'," Mariah said. "I like it here away from Master and Mistress on the island. Mistress be in my face all the time givin' me work." She picked up a handful of grass. "I do my task, then the soldier leave me alone. It a foolish idea. You go die on that river."

"But Mariah," Obi said, resting his hand on her bony

shoulder, "the island so near. How long it take to get 'cross the river?"

"It not near enough. Them big gun at the river boom you right out 'fore you leave the shore good."

Daniel and Obi looked at each other. "I goin'," Daniel said, his round face unsmiling and determined.

"An' I goin' too," Obi said firmly.

Easter deftly coiled a palm frond around the blades of grass and said nothing.

Yet, in spite of her protests, Mariah helped them, teaching Obi and Daniel how to coil the leaves around the grasses. She worked with them each evening. Every chance Easter got, she collected the grasses and palm fronds.

When October drew to a close, Obi and Daniel could work almost as swiftly and skillfully as Mariah and Easter. They'd sneak to the cove in the evenings and work on the boat by the light of a lantern. Gabriel kept watch to warn them if anyone came upon them unexpectedly.

By November, the mornings and evenings had a touch of winter chill, but the afternoons were still warm with a kind of golden, orange glow. There was little farming left to be done, and a few of the slaves had already been sent to build fortifications, dig trenches, and clear campground elsewhere.

Toward the end of November, they'd almost finished the boat. One night, Obi, Mariah, Easter, and Daniel worked together. Only a small section was left to complete.

"I glad Jameson ain't worry me with no huntin' tonight," Daniel said.

Easter nodded. "The Colonel ask me where I be till twelve. I tell him we have prayer meetin'."

"Nobody find us," Obi said. "We finish soon."

Daniel nudged Mariah, who worked next to him. "There be room for you, Mariah."

"I stayin' here. Be here too when the soldier bring y'all back."

"Someone bring a message to the Colonel today. Say there be a Yankee attack here soon," Easter said.

Daniel smiled. "That's when we get free of this camp. When them white men fight each other."

Suddenly Gabriel rushed over to them. "Someone's comin'!" he whispered.

They quickly hid the boat among the tall blades of grass. Mariah started singing a song that sounded to Obi like the dirge she sang for Buka. The rest of them clapped in time and closed their eyes as if deep in prayer.

"What y'all doin'?" It was Jameson, weaving slightly.

"Nothin', suh," Daniel said. "Just a prayer meetin'."

Jameson stared at each one. "Now, that's the dumbest thing I ever heard. Why y'all out here prayin' and singin'?"

"Sometime the spirit make us shout. Don't want to disturb nobody, suh," Gabriel said, making himself sound meek.

"Since when was you so religious, Daniel? I was lookin' for you to do some huntin'," he said.

"I pray every day the Lord send," Daniel said loudly, trying to distract him.

Obi's hands were sweating and he felt as if he had a tight band around his forehead.

Jameson faced Daniel and Obi. "Tomorrow y'all bein' sent to another camp."

Obi's head reeled. They'd have to finish the boat and leave that night.

Daniel showed no emotion. "Where we goin', suh?" he asked calmly.

"I don't know, and it ain't none of your business no way." He pulled on his beard. "Tried to get the Colonel to let you stay. You a good hunter. Gone miss you, boy."

He stumbled away from them, and when he was gone Obi pulled the boat out of the grass. "Mariah, you an' Gabriel go back to the cabin, an' Easter, you go on to the Colonel, 'fore he come lookin' for you."

"I stay a little longer," she offered.

"No, don't want nobody else comin' here. The Colonel might look for you, and if he come here, he ain't gonna be drunk like Jameson. He snoop around and find the boat."

"We come an' get you when we ready to leave," Daniel told her.

Obi and Daniel worked together until light appeared on the horizon and the gulls began their cries to the dawn. The boat was complete.

Standing up, Obi rubbed his tired fingers. He was exhausted. "I go get Easter now."

Daniel's face was weary and drawn. "Be careful. I wish we had finish this thing before it get light. Everybody gettin' up now."

"I go 'round to the back of the house. Easter be in the kitchen."

Obi walked quickly away from the cove. As he neared the cooking shed, Gabriel headed toward him.

"I just comin' for you!" he said excitedly. "You can't leave now. They's a Yankee gunboat in the river! The soldiers here is fixin' to fire them big guns."

Obi towered over the old man. "This the only chance we have," he said desperately.

"It foolhardy to get in that river now. You be blown out the water!"

"I have to, Gabriel. I goin' to get Easter."

Gabriel embraced him and shook his head sadly. "God go with you."

Obi left him and ran to the colonel's house. It had started to drizzle. The soldiers were manning the artillery at the shore. Others took positions behind the breastworks and in the trenches. No one noticed Obi dashing to the back of the house. When he reached the door that led to the kitchen, Easter came out. "Come to the woodshed," she whispered. Her eyes were frightened as they ran to the nearby shed.

"We leavin' now," Obi said nervously, holding her arms as they entered the shed. She felt small and delicate under her rough man's shirt.

Easter buried her face in his chest. He held her close to him and rested his face in her hair. "What's wrong, Easter?"

"I ain't goin', Obi," she said in a muffled voice.

"Why?' he asked hoarsely. "You still angry?"

"No, but I feel near to Jason if I stay here."

"We look for Jason together. I promise, Easter. I won't rest till I find he." He rubbed her face with one hand and held her around the waist with the other. "Suppose Wilson still lookin' for us an' find he way down here? I want us to be together."

"I do too, but I 'fraid if I go to the island, I never see Jason." She wiped her eyes. "He waitin' for us, Obi."

"Easter, we find him together. Please come with me," he pleaded.

"I stay this side of the river, Obi. Maybe a chance come for me to get to Jason."

"But then we be apart," he said sadly, still holding her to him.

"We *are* apart long as Jason not with us."

She had to tiptoe in order to rest her face on his shoulder.

"I love you, Obi. But I love Jason too. He need me. You know I here, or on the Phillips plantation, or with Master and Mistress—if they ain't gone west."

"If you don't come, then the *three* of us apart. I hear the Yankee don't turn slave away no more. Maybe we get to the Yankee an' be free."

"I never free without Jason. I never free till we three be like a family again. You understand me, Obi?"

His large, deep-set eyes stared at her intently. "No. I don't understand."

"But I understand why you have to leave. Maybe you find your ma. And these soldier—they work you to death, then they give you back to Master or sell you to someone else."

He bent down and they kissed. "I comin' back for you—and Jason—."

When he left the shed, he heard the rumble of distant thunder. He looked behind him and saw the gunboat floating in the river. Suddenly, he heard a soldier yell "Fire!" and saw black smoke spew out of the raised barrels of the artillery at the riverbank. The gunboat returned the fire. The roar of the guns mingled with the rumbling thunder, and he couldn't tell one from the other as he ran to the inlet.

Daniel looked confused. "Where Easter?" he asked when he saw Obi.

"Not comin'."

They put the boat in the inlet. "Can you swim?" Daniel asked, handing Obi a paddle.

"Why?" Obi asked, trying to steady himself in the boat.

"In case this thing don't stay on top the water."

"Can't swim," Obi yelled over the sound of exploding shells.

"I can't neither. Only know how to float."

Fortunately, the raft stayed afloat and the current helped them downriver. They stayed as close to the shore as possible. "We movin' farther from the island," Obi said nervously, taking a quick look behind him. The camp was covered with smoke.

"We can't get near the island, anyway—we get blown to pieces. Main thing is we get clear of the camp," Daniel shouted.

Obi looked to his right. Soldiers from the camp were coming to the river's edge. Daniel swore when he saw them.

"Got to go farther in the river. They comin' to hide in these reeds," he said.

They paddled as hard as they could farther out into the river.

"It's our only chance. Soldier's muskets can't reach us in the middle of the river," Daniel said, barely catching his breath. "Let's head for the gunboat."

It was beginning to rain harder. Obi knew heading for the gunboat was a crazy idea, but that seemed to be the only choice they had. His arm ached as they struggled against the current in the teeming rain. Looking at the silvery thread of water was one thing—actually being on the river was another. Obi could sense the power of the river now.

The firing stopped and the silence seemed strange. Suddenly the river became their enemy as rain fell heavily and claps of thunder rang out. The river churned under the light boat as they paddled toward the gunboat, now retreating.

Obi and Daniel were no match for the river's strength. A gust of wind caught the boat and flipped it over on top of them. Daniel reached for Obi, but Obi was carried away from his grasp.

When Obi went under, Daniel battled the river and finally grabbed Obi's head. Then he kicked, holding Obi up with one arm and waving madly with the other.

Eleven

[General] Ben Butler acted, welcoming slaves into his line, putting them to work and grandly dubbing them "contraband of war."

Lerone Bennett Jr., author
From *Before the Mayflower*

The first thing Obi noticed was the sour smell of his own damp clothes. The ground under him was wet, and for a moment he thought he was back in the swamp with Buka and Easter.

"We on the island, Obi," Daniel said when Obi opened his eyes. "The gunboat pick us up an' bring us here."

"We at the plantation?" Obi asked weakly, looking at the rows of shingled slave cabins.

"No, not at Green Hills. The gunboat drop us off at the Reynolds plantation near Green Hills." Other black people sat or lay on the ground, even though there was a slight drizzle. Some walked aimlessly up and down the narrow path between the rows of cabins.

Daniel stood up. "These people escape from the mainland too," he said. "I was waitin' for you to wake so we can go to Green Hills. That's where Buka was takin' you."

Every bone in Obi's body ached as Daniel helped him to his feet. They left the rows of cabins, Obi feeling weak and dazed. "Yankee soldier here?" Obi asked as Daniel led him past a grove of palmetto trees toward the woods.

"Yes. When the boat dock, two soldiers take all of us off an' bring us to the slave quarter." He stopped walking and shook his head.

"Let me tell you, it a good thing I eat as much food as I can find or kill, to give me strength. I carry you all the way here from the boat." Though his eyes looked tired, Daniel managed to smile a little. "You the heaviest skinny man I ever carry."

"I thought I dead when the boat turn over. You save my life."

The light rain barely seeped through the dense growth of vines and trees twisted together. Roots, almost the size of tree trunks, protruded and coiled out of the damp ground.

"Didn't want to lose you an' the boat too. Couldn't catch the boat, so I grab you," he joked.

As the woods thinned, they came to fields covered with stubble from the rice harvest and thick clods of dirt. A scattering of men trudged behind oxen, plowing the rich, dark earth. One of the men waved to them as they approached.

"That you, Daniel? How you get back?"

"Almost swim." Daniel smiled slightly, patting the man on his shoulders. "Plowin' up under the stubble, eh, Joshua?" Obi could tell that Daniel was forcing himself to be jovial.

"Daniel, Yankee come an' take over the whole island," Joshua said excitedly. "The overseers gone, Master an' Mistress gone, all the white people gone 'cept for some who hidin' in the woods from the Yankee. Yankee soldier only white people 'round here now."

"Minna an' little Daniel here?"

Obi knew immediately by the sad look in the man's eyes what the answer would be.

"They leave Green Hills. They with Master an' Mistress on the mainland."

Daniel's round face sagged. Joshua continued. "Minna ain't want to go, Daniel. First they try an' force she, but she put up a fuss. Say she have to stay here till you come back. Then Master tell she that they goin' across the river to the farm where you an' Gabriel is. I knowed they lie an' was goin' farther inland."

Obi put his arm around Daniel's broad shoulders, wishing there was something he could say to comfort his friend.

"They probably went to Master's house in Charleston," Joshua said. "Don't fret, they be fine. You see them again." Daniel stared blankly at the bleak, drizzling sky.

Obi looked around him. He wanted to ask this man if he knew a tall, black woman named Lorena, but Daniel's questions were more important for the moment.

"So many runaways come from the mainland when they learn the Yankee here. They think the Yankee go free them. They's a mess of 'em camped up in the high ground on the plantation. The soldier tell us to do our usual task. Say now we grow rice for the Treasury Department, whatever that be," he said, shaking his head. "Them Yankee soldier don't know nothin' about runnin' no plantation."

Daniel looked dazed. "My cabin gone too?"

Joshua nodded. "We tell the Yankee don't put nobody new in there 'cause that cabin belongs to somebody. But they don't listen. Say they needs someplace to put all the fugitive peoples." He tugged gently at Daniel's sleeve. "Come, rice in the pot. You and your friend eat somethin'." Joshua had his small, three-legged iron skillet in the field with him.

He smiled kindly at Obi. "You an' your friend can sleep in my cabin till you find someplace."

"You a kind man, Joshua. Where you find room for us when you have a wife an' four children?"

He shrugged his shoulders. "We find a chink of space for you on the floor."

Thanking him, Daniel said, "We go to the quarter an'

find a place to clean ourselves and rest." They left the rice fields and walked along the supply canal used for flooding the fields during the growing season.

"I know this happen, Obi," Daniel said as they continued walking. "Slave don't have nothin' belong to he—not he woman, child, cabin—not even he self."

When they reached higher ground, Obi couldn't believe his eyes. Green Hills was twice the size of the Phillips plantation.

Behind the large, two-story family house, with its porch running almost its entire width, stood stables, barns, a lake, and a terraced garden. Another field, where peas, okra, corn, and other crops were grown, ran parallel to the family house and ended near the slave quarters.

An avenue of oak trees shaded the large lawn that led to the house. Blue-coated men milled about the lawns and gardens. Tents in the background reminded Obi of the camp they'd just left. Obi stared at the soldiers, realizing this was the first time he was seeing a Yankee in the flesh.

They headed for the slave quarter but were stopped by two soldiers posted at the edge of the field, just beyond the row of cabins.

The men watched Obi and Daniel as they approached. "All fugitives have to report to the superintendent and the captain."

"Then you have to go to the camp with the other fugitives," the second soldier added.

Obi and Daniel looked at each other, both of them having trouble understanding what the soldiers were saying.

"I live here, but my cabin give away to someone else, suh."

Now the soldiers stared at Obi and Daniel as if they didn't understand them. Obi was thinking that the biggest difference between the Yankees and the southern whites was the way the Yankees talked. It sounded as if the words were trapped inside their noses.

Daniel tried to explain again. "Suh, we not runaways. We belong to Master Turner."

A portly older man with long, red sideburns came toward them from the direction of the fields. Instead of a uniform, he wore a black frock coat.

"More fugitives?" he asked, peering closely at Daniel and Obi.

"They claim they belong here," the soldier said. "At least I think that's what they're saying."

"We not runaways. We belong to Master Turner, suh," Daniel sighed wearily.

The man in the frock coat talked slowly to Obi and Daniel, as if he were addressing very young children. "Your master is a traitor. The United States government therefore has seized any property belonging to him. Do you understand?"

Obi didn't understand and neither did Daniel.

"Suh, you returnin' me to Master Turner?" Daniel asked patiently.

"I just told you," the man said calmly. "Your master is our enemy. Anything that belongs to him, we have the right to take."

Now Obi understood. "We ain't free, then, suh?" Daniel asked.

"That's not for me to say."

Daniel stared intently at the man. "We belong to you, suh?"

The man's face reddened. "No. You belong to the Treasury Department."

Obi recalled that the man in the field had also mentioned this Treasury Department thing. Obi wondered what it was.

"I have to get back to the mainland, suh, to find my wife an' baby."

"What? I don't understand. You—"

"Master send me to work for the Confederates. Then he leave an' take my wife an' baby with he."

"You were at the camp on the other side of the river?" The man stared intently at Daniel as if he didn't want to miss a word he said. "You were both there?"

"Yes, suh," Daniel answered.

"Could you tell us how many artillery there are? And men?"

"Yes, suh. I know all that."

The man looked at the soldiers. "Maybe the captain could use these two."

"Maybe," one of the soldiers said. "These blacks know the territory. Maybe they could show us where there's a weak spot in the Rebel shore defense."

Obi lost interest in the conversation. He wanted to eat, sleep, and then scour the island and find Lorena.

The man looked at Obi. "What do you know about this area?"

"Don't know nothin', suh," Obi answered.

Daniel continued. "Suh, can I go to find my wife an' baby?"

"I think that's dangerous."

"I know how to find my way, suh."

"Could you guide someone through these swamps?"

"Yes, suh. Know them well."

The man turned to Obi. "Could you do the same?"

"No, suh. Don't know about no swamp nor how to do nothin'."

"These slavers wouldn't have you if you didn't know anything," he snapped.

"He a first-rate carpenter, suh," Daniel said.

Obi glared at him. He didn't want these men to know what he could do. He wasn't going to be around here for long. Daniel reminded him of Easter's letting the Colonel know that she was a cook.

"We may need carpenters," the man said quickly. "But until that time comes, you go with the others tomorrow to the rice field."

"And you," he said, turning to Daniel, "come and see me. Superintendent James. Got that?"

Daniel nodded. "Yes, suh, but I have to go back to the mainland."

"Well, maybe we can help each other. You come see me and the Captain tomorrow."

Daniel nodded. "Yes, suh, Super . . . Super . . ."

The soldiers laughed at him.

Got a nerve to laugh, funny as they talk, Obi thought.

"Superintendent James," the man repeated.

"Yes, suh," Daniel mumbled.

"The slave quarter is filled up," the man said. "You'll have to stay in the camp with the others." He pointed beyond the terraced garden to an area Obi hadn't noticed before. There were makeshift shelters—sticks with pieces of old cloth and canvas thrown over them—lean-tos with canvas over the space where a door would normally have been, and a few stick-and-mud shacks.

Instead of going to the camp behind the garden, Daniel walked silently to the slave quarter, and Obi followed. Daniel stopped in front of a small, weather-beaten cabin. "That was our cabin," he muttered sadly.

Obi felt too sorry for Daniel, too weary, to be excited about finally reaching the island. He missed Easter, Buka, and Jason too. They should all be there with him. After all the years of planning and dreaming of breaking free, he still felt like Obi, the slave of John Jennings.

Twelve

*The sons of thousands of white mothers were dying,
and people were beginning to say that blacks could
stop bullets as well as white men.*

Lerone Bennett Jr., author
From *Before the Mayflower*

May 1862

Imitating the movements of the other men and women in
the field, Obi dropped the rice seeds into the small trench
and, with his bare foot, covered it over with dirt. He repeated the same process at the next trench, about twelve
inches away.

The songs of the yellow and black rice birds created a
kind of music to accompany the sowers' "dance" across the
field. Obi looked anxiously at the position of the sun. It
was about four o'clock—only a few more hours to work.

For five months now, Obi had spent his free time search-
ing for Lorena. He'd managed to talk to the older slaves at
Green Hills, as well as the slaves on the other plantations
on the island.

Until yesterday, no one had heard of his mother. Yesterday, however, he'd found an old woman who'd told him
that yes, she'd definitely known Lorena and that Lorena
had been sold years ago to a plantation on another island.

Obi hoped that Daniel would return this evening. He

needed to talk to him. He felt he should leave Green Hills so that he could continue his search for his mother, but he wanted to talk to Daniel first. Daniel had been working as a guide for the captain. He led small groups of soldiers through the swamps so that they could gather information and draw accurate maps of the coastal areas. Recently his assignment was more dangerous.

Given false papers stating that he was free, he travelled back and forth to the mainland, reporting on Confederate troop movements. Several times he'd sneaked to the camp to visit Easter, Mariah, and Gabriel before he returned to the island.

The first time he returned from the camp, he had told Obi, "Easter say the Colonel think we drown in the river."

On his last assignment, he had stopped at the camp again. "Easter say she miss you," he informed Obi. "I workin' on her. I tell her the Yankee tell you to do your task, then he leave you be. Least he ain't buyin' an' sellin' your hide."

"What she say?" Obi asked.

"Say she think on it. I sneak her out of there easy, Obi."

When Obi wasn't thinking about Lorena, he thought about Easter. His mind kept drawing the same pictures: Easter as a little, barefoot girl in shirttails; Easter growing into a young woman. But the image that gave him the most pain and guilt was Easter crying because Jason was no longer with her.

Maybe Daniel would bring Easter with him this evening when he returned. When the sun finally began to set, Obi and the other field hands trudged back to the slave quarter. Obi shared a hastily built shack with a group of other young men who didn't have families. He didn't like sleeping in the crude shelter with so many others, but it was better than being in the squalid camp behind the garden.

As he walked toward the cabin, he saw Daniel waving to him. Obi was relieved. Each time Daniel left Green Hills, Obi wondered whether his friend would return safely. Before Obi could say hello, Daniel practically pounced on him.

"Obi! I hear the General freein' us. Say if we join the army, we get freedom paper an' ten dollars a month pay."

Obi sat down wearily on the ground in front of the shack.

"What general?" he asked.

"The general who the boss of all these islands," he said, sitting next to him. "He at Port Royal, another island to the south of us. He startin' a black regiment." His round face burst into a wide grin. "I been hopin' for this all these months. I want to get into this fight too!"

"I don't want to be soldier or slave. This ain't none of my war. I goin' to find my mother. That's what I want to tell you. A woman tell me that Lorena sent to another island."

"What island?"

"She ain't know that."

Daniel's face became serious. "Your ma is a dream of the past, Obi. I bet you don't even remember she face." He gazed sadly at the purple sky. "Pick up a gun an' fight these slavers. Then you find Easter an' the boy. That the future." He pointed his index finger in Obi's face as if he were aiming a gun.

"You crazy," Obi responded. "I never know why you come back here when you have paper sayin' you free. You should find Minna an' take she an' little Daniel to Mexico."

"I like it fine on this island," Daniel said. "May not like Mexico. I joinin' the regiment. And I go fight my way out this slavery mess. Piece of this land be mine, an' me an' Minna have a *real* marriage—not a slave marriage, where Master sell you, your wife, an' child."

"I don't trust these Yankee, Daniel. I think whoever win the war keep us. No, I have to find Lorena, get Easter an' Jason. Then we all leavin' this land of slaves."

Obi noticed that Daniel avoided his eyes when he mentioned Easter. "You see her this time?" he asked.

Daniel sighed. "The Colonel gone an' Easter leave with he. They's only about fifty soldiers at the shore now, an' a new colonel. Gabriel an' Mariah an' a few field hands still there."

Daniel grinned, but Obi knew that he was just trying to cheer him up. "The Colonel and Easter not far. Just a different camp, I sure. I find out where they be. Next time I come back, I bringin' Easter with me." He patted Obi on his back. "Another thing happen. I find where Minna stayin' in Charleston."

"You see her?" Obi asked dully, his mind still on Easter.

"Not yet, but I get there an' I bringin' them back here with me."

"It be dangerous." Obi looked at his friend, his eyes large and sad.

"I know, but I gettin' them anyway. An' I gonna pick up a rifle an' show them slavers that I a man too."

As the month of May wore on, the heat of the sun grew more intense. Daniel and a few of the other men on the plantation joined the black regiment. Obi wanted to continue his search for Lorena, but Daniel persuaded him to stay on the island a while longer.

One evening, as they ate supper in the communal eating area near the cooking shed, Daniel said, "I a army man, but I still do my same job. I leavin' tomorrow, Obi, an' I comin' back with Minna, little Daniel, an' Easter." He smiled and scooped up a spoonful of rice. "I be gone a little longer this time. Ain't leavin' Charleston without Minna an' the baby. I a soldier now," he said proudly.

"Be careful. Rebels say you a slave—not a soldier," Obi said.

Daniel grinned as if he didn't have a care in the world. "My hide be wide an' strong."

"Them Rebel shells be wider an' stronger," Obi warned.

Daniel rested his spoon on the plate. "Don't go runnin' off nowhere till I get back, Obi. I bringin' them women with me. Maybe I even pick up Gabriel an' that hardhead, Mariah, an' bring them back too."

Daniel left the next morning. Obi watched sadly as his friend walked toward the river, where the ferry would take him to the mainland. He almost ran after him, to tell him again to be careful.

Obi worked the rice fields and waited impatiently for Daniel's return. A few more men joined the black regiment, but not Obi.

In the sweltering evenings as he walked from the rice fields to the quarter, he barely noticed the ex–field hands, still in overalls and straw hats. They were being drilled by a soldier on what used to be the well-kept lawn in front of the family house.

By the middle of July, when the rice was beginning to ripen, Daniel had not yet returned. Obi began to worry. He'd sit by the wharf when he wasn't working and look for the familiar face among the fugitives who were still escaping in droves to the Sea islands.

On a burning mid-August afternoon, while Obi pulled the weeds from around the rice plants, he thought he heard someone calling him. Looking toward the edge of the field, he saw a man he knew approaching him.

"Obi," the man yelled excitedly, "Daniel been kilt."

"You lie, man!" Obi cried.

"No," the man said, "a soldier tell me when I sell he the eggs his mornin'. Rebels shoot he. Find out he spyin' for the Yankee."

Obi felt like flying into a rage, but just as suddenly he felt empty, as if life had been drained out of him also. The man shook his head sadly. "Son, better time comin'."

Obi left the field and walked back to the quarter. He sat on the ground in front of the shack where he and Daniel had often sat and talked in the evenings. *Lorena gone. Easter an' Jason gone. Buka dead. Daniel dead. Everything dead.* He didn't cry outwardly, but inside, the tears flowed like the river when the floodgates were opened onto the rice fields.

Over the familiar cries of birds and the sounds of hammering and horses whinnying, he heard the shrill voice of the drillmaster. Recalling how slaves helped one another complete their tasks, Obi stood up. He had to complete Daniel's job now.

Obi walked toward the big house. Moving with precision, the soldiers of the black regiment drilled on the lawn. They wore a uniform of dark-blue trousers and wide, black hats. Obi stepped up to the young, white soldier who assisted the drillmaster.

"Suh," he said softly, "I joinin' those men."

"Sorry, feller. This regiment is about to be disbanded," he said.

Obi was confused, "Suh?" he asked.

"Orders from Washington. The Captain gave us the news today. Said that there'll be no black regiments in the army, but now you fellers will be paid when you work for us."

Obi watched the men turning left, then right as they followed the drillmaster's orders.

"This is the last drill for them," the soldier said as he watched the men. Then he turned to Obi. "Don't look so downhearted, feller. You're free as long as you're on our territory. You'll be earning a wage too." He smiled pleasantly.

Obi walked back to the quarter. He didn't have the energy to figure out what the soldier meant, except that there would be no black soldiers in the Union Army. *Daniel die for nothin' an' I can't help him.*

As he trudged along the oak-lined lawn, he wiped the sweat running down his smooth face. Even the trees couldn't offer shade from the fiery August sun.

Instead of going to the fields the next morning, he headed toward the river. He'd collect the reeds and palm leaves he needed in order to make another boat and continue to look for Lorena. He pulled up a few long reeds and then stopped. Making a boat only made him feel worse about Easter and Daniel.

A man who had been in the black regiment walked over to him. "You gonna work for the Yankees too?" he asked.

A flock of rice birds flew above them. "Yankee don't want us for soldier. I goin' south to Mexico, just like them bird," he said quietly.

"The drillmaster say they go start another regiment. In the meantime, I goin' to the wharf an' make some money. Yankee hirin' men to load an' unload the boats an' supply wagons."

Obi left the reeds where he'd dropped them and walked along the riverbank with the man. Maybe Daniel was right. Lorena was the past. He had to think about the future.

"We get pay for work? We get real money?" Obi asked.

"Yes. No more slave for someone else. No more workin' for nothin'."

Obi stayed on the island and worked as a stevedore for the Union Army, loading and unloading boats. Not a day went by that he didn't think about Easter and Daniel. Slowly he came to believe that if the Yankees won the war, then slavery would be dead too. He began to think like Daniel and wanted to help make sure the Yankees won.

As 1862 drew to an end, a rumor spread through the plantation like the winter rains. President Lincoln was going to sign a paper declaring all slaves free.

Thirteen

Nor are they lazy, either about work or drill; in all respects they seem better material for soldiers than I had dared to hope.

Colonel Thomas W. Higginson,
December 3, 1862
From *Army Life in a Black Regiment*

1863

It was a chilly New Year's Day when the captain summoned everyone to the plantation lawn so that he could tell them about the paper the President had signed.

Standing tall and pale on the steps of the family house, he made the announcement. "The paper says that all slaves in those states fighting us are now free."

Suppose there were slaves in places that didn't fight the Yankees, Obi mused. *Were they free too? Was Easter an' Jason free now? Maybe the Yankees only fought people who had slaves.* A young woman standing near Obi crossed her arms as the wind blew her tattered shawl.

"Captain, suh," she called out, "do them slave-drivin' Rebels know 'bout this paper?"

"That's what I thinkin' too," a man behind Obi mumbled.

The captain hesitated for a moment before he answered. "The Confederacy knows, but they're rebelling against us, and that's why we're fighting," he answered, fingering the gold-colored sash around his waist.

The same young woman spoke up again. "If them Rebels come an' take this island back, we be slave again?"

Before the captain could respond, another man called out. "Suh, in other words, them Rebels ain't payin' that paper no mind, is they?"

The captain cleared his throat as his face started to color. "We'll make them pay it some mind," he said.

Everyone began to talk at the same time. Obi wondered whether this news meant that he could go to the mainland and bring Easter and Jason to the island. He didn't have the nerve to question the captain like the others did. Anyway, he reasoned, the Rebels weren't freeing anyone, and Easter and Jason were in Rebel territory.

The captain held up a thin hand. "Quiet. I have more news. All able-bodied men of African descent will be allowed to join the military."

Obi smiled slowly while some of the men cheered. *Now I finish Daniel's task.*

On a rainy, dreary morning two weeks after the captain's announcement, Obi was on a ferry with about thirty other men from Green Hills Plantation. They were headed for the training camp at another Sea island off the Carolina coast.

Obi and some of the others leaned over the boat's railing as the ferry pulled out from the island. A few of the men waved to friends and relatives who'd come to the wharf to see them off. Obi's mind was on Daniel, wishing that they were making this trip together.

Obi touched his breast, checking to see if the pouch containing his twenty-four dollars was still pinned to the inside of his jacket. He'd earned the money during the five months he'd worked for the army. Money for him, Easter, and Jason when they began their new life together.

When the boat reached the landing at Hilton Head Island, they left the ferry and were led by two white soldiers to the camp. Obi remembered the Confederate camp by the river as they passed the cabins and soldiers' tents. Some soldiers were already being drilled, and others were learning how to use the artillery. Obi's group was brought to a long, well-built log house that stood beside several frame buildings.

The log house had one large room. A few black men sat on benches lining the walls. Several other blacks stood in front of a white soldier who sat behind a desk covered with papers.

Another soldier sat at a desk in a far corner of the room. A couple of young white troops lounged on the edge of his desk, watching the new black recruits.

"Line up behind these men," one of the soldiers ordered.

While Obi stood on line, he looked around the bare room. The white soldiers at the corner desk watched the scene with amused smiles.

Obi was startled when the soldier behind the desk yelled, "Next!" The other men from Obi's group had finished being questioned by the man. They sat together on several benches.

Obi stepped up to the desk.

"Your name?" he asked gruffly.

"Obi, suh."

"Your full name."

"Obidiah, suh." He still had to listen carefully to understand Yankee talk.

"I mean full name. Two names. First and last."

"Only have one, suh."

"Mother Mary," the man mumbled. "I mean family name. Ain't you got a family name?"

"No, suh. Got no family."

"What was your master's name?"

Obi hesitated before answering. "John Jennings, suh."

"That'll be your name, then." The man wrote quickly on a piece of paper. "You're now Private Obidiah Jennings."

"Suh, that's not my family. My mother name Lorena."

"Doesn't count," he said impatiently, handing Obi a piece of paper. "Take a seat until you're called."

"But suh, my name ain't Jennings," Obi insisted, clenching his fist.

"That's what it is now!" he shouted. "Move on! We ain't got all day!"

The room became quiet except for a loud laugh from one of the white soldiers.

A man from the group that had been on the boat with Obi left the bench and approached him. "It don't mean nothin'. I use Master Turner name. Now I John Turner."

"I ain't care what you use. My name ain't Jennings!" Obi snapped. John shrugged his shoulders and sat down again.

Another man who'd also been on the boat said, "I use my mother name. Chaney. I Joseph Chaney. Go an' tell the man to change it to your ma's name."

There was a long line of men still waiting their turn. Obi was too angry and embarrassed to go back to the man. He turned to the men on the bench. "None of you better call me that name. My name's Obi."

He plopped down angrily on a bench by himself and turned the paper he'd been given upside down and right side up, then front to back. His head throbbed as he looked at the man again and then at the paper he couldn't read. Maybe it wasn't such a good idea to join the army. Maybe he should have stuck to his original plans. He angrily crumpled the paper into a ball.

"Don't tear it up. You may need it."

Obi looked at the speaker and couldn't respond at first because he thought he was seeing and hearing things. A black man he'd seen when they entered the room stood over him. Obi couldn't believe he was hearing Yankee sounds coming out of this man's full mouth.

"What's that you be sayin'?" Obi asked.

The man sat down next to Obi. "My name's Thomas

West." He put out his hand. Obi, still staring, shook Thomas's hand slowly.

"My name Obi," he finally responded. Though he knew it was impolite, he couldn't stop staring at the man. Even though his heavy trousers and jacket were old and worn, he didn't look like a field hand, nor did he look like an ex-slave house servant.

"How you learn that Yankee talk?" Obi asked.

"I was born in New York."

"New York?" Obi looked puzzled.

"A northern city."

"Oh. You free colored?" Buka had told Obi about free blacks in the North. Buka was the only "free colored" Obi had known personally.

"Who was you master before you free?"

"Never had one," Thomas replied, looking down at the crumpled paper in Obi's hand. "You'll probably need that paper. Shows that you're in the army." Thomas watched Obi intently with wide eyes.

"I saw you turning the paper back and forth. Can't you read?" he asked cautiously, not wanting to offend Obi.

"No," Obi said, avoiding Thomas's eyes and handing him the ball of paper. "What it say?"

Thomas smoothed the paper in his lap and read: "Private Obidiah Jennings. United States Army. Regiment: First South Carolina Volunteers; Company B. January 15, 1863." He handed Obi the paper. "This is for identification."

"How you learn to read?"

"In the colored orphanage where my mother worked. I went to school with the orphans."

Obi looked puzzled again. Thomas explained what an orphan was.

"That's what I be," Obi said. "No ma, no pa. You know your mother an' father?"

Thomas nodded his large head. "My daddy is dead now. He was a slave, but he ran away to the North when he was a boy."

"Why you join the army? You already free," Obi said.

"Not so free. We don't have masters but don't have any rights either." Thomas nervously swung one crossed leg back and forth. "We figure if slavery is ended, then all of us blacks will be free." He smiled. "Anyway, thirteen dollars a month is more than I get working in the stables or on the docks, when I can find work there."

Obi listened for a moment to the voices of Joseph, John, and the others who'd been on the ferry. Obi liked this man from the North. He reminded him of Buka. Like the old African, Thomas could tell Obi about places and things he knew nothing about.

"Could you learn me to read?" he asked shyly.

Thomas smiled. "Sure. Be glad to, Obi."

"Everybody stand and form a single line," the soldier behind the desk ordered. Feeling calmer now, Obi was sorry that his talk with Thomas had to end.

They slowly formed a line. Obi and Thomas stood behind Joseph and John.

The sergeant, short and straight as a board, stepped from behind his desk. "The first thing you've got to learn is how to follow orders quickly." He tapped his index finger on his forehead. "Soldiers have to react fast. I'm Sergeant Michaels. Your commanding officer, Colonel Higginson, will speak to you later. Now follow me."

Michaels walked them out of the log house and toward one of the frame buildings.

Joseph imitated his short steps. "He strut like a little bantam rooster," he snickered.

The sergeant stopped in front of the building and faced the men. "We're going to try and make you *look* like soldiers," he announced before leading them inside the building.

Inside, Obi noticed little other than the neatly placed pairs of boots in one section.

Thomas looked down at his own scruffy boots. "Good boots. One reason for joining the army, Obi," he joked.

Obi grimaced at the thought of wearing them. The men started talking at once. "After you pick your boots, go over there and get your uniforms." Michaels pointed to the other side of the room where a black man was measuring a few soldiers.

Obi picked up the largest pair of boots he could find. "It's not good to wear shoes that are too big," Thomas advised loudly.

Joseph, John, and the others stopped talking. They stared at Thomas. "Well, I'll be," John exclaimed.

Joseph grinned. "Where you learn to talk like that?" he asked, and the other men laughed.

"He must've been 'round them Yankee a long time," another said.

"Y'all leave he alone," Obi ordered.

John turned to him. "You sure enough in a evil mood, Obi. We only funnin' with he."

"It doesn't matter," Thomas said to Obi. "Better find yourself a decent pair of boots." As Thomas picked through the boots, he told the others where he was from and patiently answered their questions. By the time they left the building, even Obi had to laugh when John said, "I never thought there was such a thing as a colored Yankee!"

After they got their uniforms, the sergeant marched them to the tents where they'd be quartered. In the distance, Obi saw other tents and cabins for the white soldiers.

Beyond, Obi spotted the familiar big, white house and the rows of slave cabins with little black children playing in front of them. Black women walked gracefully with baskets balanced on their heads. The camp was on a former plantation.

Obi, Thomas, John, Joseph, and a young-looking boy named Henry shared a tent. It had been a long day. Obi placed his clothing and the dreaded boots in the corner next to his pallet and lay down.

The men continued to tease Thomas, who took their ribbing good-naturedly. Then they teased Obi because he was the only one who hadn't tried on his boots. "Y'all don't leave me be, them boots gonna be sittin' top your heads," he said, not really as angry as he tried to sound. In fact, Obi was beginning to feel quite pleased with himself. He agreed with Joseph, who said, "I ain't sure why these white men be fightin' each other, but we fightin' for we freedom."

It seemed that as soon as he fell off to sleep, the sound of a bugle woke him up. They dressed in the cold tent. Obi stood up in his blue trousers, jacket, and forage cap, snugly fitting his head. As they started to leave the tent, Joseph stared at Obi's feet. "Where your boot, man?" he asked.

Wiggling his toes in his black socks, Obi said, "These be fine with me."

Joseph picked up one of Obi's boots and pointed it at him as if it were a gun. Thomas and the others laughed. John shivered as he pulled on his cap. "Better leave Obi alone. He don't like he name or he boots."

Joseph grabbed Obi's other boot and tossed it to Thomas. "Here, I need help. This go be a big battle."

Obi backed away from them, smiling and frowning at the same time. Joseph leaped quickly and tackled Obi to the ground. Henry held Obi down while Thomas and Joseph stuffed his feet into the boots.

The men laughed so much that Obi had to force himself to keep an annoyed face. A smile played around his mouth. "Y'all payin' for this. 'Specially you, Thomas. Next time they poke fun at you, I joinin' 'em."

Laughter followed Obi as he limped out of the tent to the field where the men were lining up for roll call.

Private Jennings didn't learn to like his name or his boots, but he, along with the other men of Company B, adjusted well to military life. Sergeant Michaels noticed how fast Obi learned how to handle the artillery. "Private, you've done this before?" he asked one day after their instruction.

"No, suh. I seen it at the Rebel camp," Obi answered.

"There's a couple of men I want you to help. They'll get

shot to bits while they load if they don't learn to do it faster."

Besides the drilling and instruction, Company B was to clear more campground, build cabins, unload ships, cook, clean, and do sentry duty.

In March they were sent to Jacksonville, Florida, to help hold that captured city. In April they returned to South Carolina. They took part in skirmishes and in expeditions along the coastal rivers.

A year passed. They worked hard, even though they were paid only seven dollars a month, instead of the thirteen dollars they'd been promised.

Over the months, Obi's friendship with the men grew—especially with Thomas. Many nights, while the other men relaxed around the campfires, Thomas stayed in the tent with Obi, teaching him the sounds of the alphabet. They had no books, so Thomas used the letters his mother sent from time to time. As he helped Obi read her words, Obi felt as if the letters were also meant for him.

In February 1864, Obi, Thomas, Joseph, and a few of the others in the regiment were transferred to black units in Tennessee. The morning that they left, they stood waving from the deck of the ship that would carry them from the island to the mainland.

The rest of the men in their company, and even Sergeant Michaels, had come to see them off. Obi stood erect, his blue jacket perfectly fitted to his long, slender body and his haversack strapped across his back.

Thomas was next to Obi, his boots polished to a high shine. Joseph wore his cap turned slightly to the side, and he waved a clenched fist.

The boat pulled away from the dock, and the island slowly disappeared from view. Obi realized that he'd miss the men and the camp and that his new life would take him even farther from the life and the people he had always known.

Fourteen

We knew [General Forrest] was in our Country. We knew he had just butchered Fort Pillow.

From the diary of James T. Ayers,
Civil War Recruiter
May 10, 1864

April 12–13, 1864

The last traces of dark sky disappeared. Obi's thoughts returned to the present as the town began to wake. The blacksmith entered his shop, and the young child who worked at the general store was outside, sweeping the ground in front of the entrance. Several soldiers from the Thirteenth Tennessee Battalion talked and laughed loudly while walking down the bluff toward the river.

The bobwhites called to one another, and the sounds of laughter blended with the clanging blacksmith's hammer. The odor of wood smoke and new grass reminded Obi of the Jennings farm.

Out of habit, Obi patted his breast, making sure the pouch was there. Black soldiers were now receiving the thirteen dollars a month they'd been promised, and Obi had saved sixty dollars.

Leaning back on the steps with his hands behind his head, Thomas swung one of his crossed legs nervously from side to side. His wide eyes scanned the pale, blue sky.

"Looks like a nice spring day, Obi."

Obi glanced at the gunboat floating peacefully in the river. "I hope it stay nice," he mumbled.

"Don't worry. As I said before, Rebels try and climb this hill, we can swat them down like flies."

Suddenly they heard gunfire. It seemed as if the birds, the hammering, and the soldiers' laughter ceased at once. Obi and Thomas grabbed their guns and sprang to their feet. The pickets in the woods were running for cover in the fort. "General Forrest here," Obi whispered hoarsely. "They attackin' the fort!"

Instead of remaining at his post, Obi ran toward the fort. He scarcely heard Thomas calling his name or the noise when Thomas fired his rifle. These sounded far away to Obi. He stumbled over small rocks, branches, and logs as he ran. The hill had never seemed so steep or difficult to climb. Less than one quarter of the way up the hill, Obi heard Thomas calling him again.

Then Obi saw the Confederate soldiers in their butternut-colored uniforms streaming out of the hollow above the fort. He froze in panic. In that split second he recalled something said to Buka so many months ago: "Old man, you live this long 'cause you had sense enough not to fight no white man."

Thomas jerked Obi hard and he came to his senses. Before they turned to run back down to the river, the cluster of men rushing toward them were scattered by a shell from one of the Yankee guns.

Thomas and Obi almost slid down the hill on their backs as they tried to run to their post. They hit the ground when a minié ball whizzed over their heads. Yellow and black smoke from the guns darkened the rising sun while screams and shouts merged with the roar of the artillery.

They crawled to the two frame buildings. The boy who had been sweeping earlier lay face up on the ground between the buildings. Obi started to reach for him, then saw that the youngster was dead, half of his face a red, pulpy mass.

By now, Rebel troops were swarming like bees out of the ravines while the Union gunboat in the river shelled them from one ravine to the other.

Thomas and Obi dashed to the general store. They both tumbled into the building, crashing into some barrels near the door. As Thomas tried to load his rifle, his hands trembled so much that Obi had to do it for him.

"It done the same way we learn. No different," Obi said, handing Thomas the gun. "I get scare too."

"Don't know what happened. Got nervous all of a sudden," Thomas muttered, looking embarrassed.

Obi crept under an open window that faced the cabins. "This a good spot to shoot from if any Rebs come out of them woods behind the cabins." He scrunched in the corner and placed the barrel of his rifle on the windowsill.

Thomas guarded the entrance. They shot at Rebel soldiers who tried to step out of the woods. At about three o'clock the firing stopped. The silence itself seemed loud after all the shelling and gunfire.

"We need to find out what's happening," Thomas said. Obi's heart banged against his chest as they left the store. They looked around them carefully, walking toward the frame buildings. Obi tried not to stare at the bodies of the dead.

"You boys held your ground. Good soldiers."

Obi spun around and looked in the face of Sergeant Johnson, the Driver. "Everybody ordered inside the fort. Major Booth was killed at eight o'clock this morning," he said, trying not to show any emotion. The sergeant rubbed his hands together as he talked. "Rebels flyin' two flags of truce. Forrest send a message to Major Bradford that he want the fort to surrender."

"Sarge, if we surrender, you know what happen to us?" Obi asked angrily. "Rebels either kill us or put us back in chains." White officers, as well as their black troops, were threatened with death if captured.

"Don't worry," he said, trying to sound cheerful, "the Major won't surrender." He started walking away. "Let me round up the rest of the boys."

Obi and Thomas climbed the hill to the fort. Bodies of Confederate soldiers were scattered along the crest of the hill. A wounded Union soldier, holding his arm, came out of the cabin that was used as a hospital.

When they entered the fort, they found many of the townspeople taking refuge inside. The girl who reminded Obi of Easter sat in a corner of the floor with her little brother. Her two other brothers—the ones Obi and Thomas called the little generals—ran back and forth with water for the soldiers.

The blacksmith and the man who owned the general store talked quietly, leaning against the wall. Obi and Thomas climbed one of the ladders to the top of the fort. Joseph was at his gun, talking to the other artillerymen.

He greeted Obi and Thomas, and then, leaning over the parapet, he pointed at the gunboat, now in the middle of the river. "She out there coolin' off and cleanin' her guns. We run them Rebs right off this hill."

Obi surveyed the trees and brush on either side of the hill and the ravines above and below the fort. "I bet Rebs be all in them woods. While them flags flyin' for truce, they sneakin' closer to the fort," he said.

"The first flag of truce just went down," another gunner informed them, pointing to a Confederate cavalryman at the bottom of the hill, holding a white flag.

A few moments later a lieutenant climbed up the ladder. "We're not surrendering the fort. Prepare to fire!" They all cheered. Obi looked again at the cavalryman. After a few minutes, the second flag was taken down and an avalanche of Confederate soldiers fell upon the fort.

Obi and Thomas quickly climbed down and ran to the powder magazine to get more ammunition. When they reached the lower level, they stopped. Civilians and the

Union soldiers alike were racing out of the fort. Some of the soldiers had dropped their weapons and had their hands raised in surrender.

Joining the others, Thomas and Obi left the fort. Confederate soldiers were all over the hill, some yelling, "No quarter! Give them no quarter!" Smoke came from the direction of the town. There were shouts and screams from men, women, and children as the Confederate troops opened fire.

Obi and Thomas were fleeing down the hill when Thomas was hit. He fell, dropping his rifle and grabbing his leg. Obi dragged him to the hospital cabin. Three nurses—two white and one black—were still tending to the wounded.

The black nurse saw them enter and came over to them. Rolling up Thomas's trouser leg, she looked at his wound. "Looks bad, and the surgeon ain't here. Best I can do now is bandage you up. If the pain gets too bad, I try and take the ball out myself."

Thomas groaned. The woman took some bandages off a cabinet and handed them to Obi. "Wrap him up. Stop some of that bleeding. Got a man over there worse off than he is." She pointed to a stocky form sprawled on the floor, breathing heavily. It was Sergeant Johnson.

Obi quickly tied Thomas's wound as his friend gritted his teeth in pain. *He need a surgeon bad.* When Obi finished, Thomas said, "I can't move. You go on. Maybe you can get to the gunboat or hide in the woods. I'll be fine here." His eyes looked dazed. "I'll only hold you back."

Obi shook his head. "I stay with you."

"Go, Obi," he barely whispered. "Nurse fix me up and get me through. I know we'll get reinforcements here soon."

"Can't leave you, Thomas."

"Help will come. I know it. You go on. Remember that girl, Easter, is waiting for you. And that little boy."

Obi stood up and walked to the door. He hesitated.

"Go on, Obi. Nurse will patch me up."

Obi couldn't look back as he left the hospital. Stepping over bodies, he raced toward the woods on the river side of the fort. He felt like a disloyal coward. Thomas had been a good friend. But maybe Thomas was right. Union reinforcements would come and all would be well.

Obi found a tangle of vines and brush and hid himself from the Confederate cavalrymen who rode up and down the bluff, taking some people as prisoners and shooting others.

He made a small space so that he could see what was happening along the hillside. When things quieted down, he would escape to the river. Peering out of his shelter, he saw one of the cavalrymen on his horse motion for the little "generals" to come toward him. The boys took short, hesitant steps, and the soldier shot them point blank.

Though it could give his hiding place away, Obi aimed his rifle and fired at the soldier. The man slumped over his horse as the animal bucked and took off down the hill. There was so much noise, smoke, and confusion that Obi's action went unnoticed.

Before he could reload, he saw flames flare up near the cabin hospital. He quickly loaded his last bit of ammunition and left the shelter. He had to get Thomas out of the cabin. *Can't leave Thomas like I leave Jason,* he told himself. *Thomas would stay right there with me.*

Fortunately, the thick smoke was a good cover, but he had to be careful. When he heard shouting nearby, he lay face down next to the lifeless form of another black soldier.

"He's a goner," a voice drawled. Obi felt himself being turned over and summoned all the control he had when the man reached in his jacket and removed the pouch with his money and papers. He also took his rifle. When the man left, Obi staggered through the smoke and entered the hospital.

Heavy smoke made it almost impossible to see. There

wasn't a sound. "Thomas? Thomas?" Obi yelled and coughed. He felt around the floor where he'd left his friend. He pulled someone's arm. "Thomas?"

"Obi? That you?" a voice cried weakly. "They came in here and killed everyone. They took me for dead."

"I gettin' you out."

"I can't move."

"Yes, you can." Thomas grunted as Obi pulled him up. "Put your arm around my shoulder and hop on your good leg."

Coughing and choking, they left the room as one of the walls caved in, consumed by fire. Moving as fast as Thomas could go on one foot, they hobbled through the confusion of soldiers, civilians, horses, and dead bodies to the wooded area where Obi had been.

The girl, the one who reminded Obi of Easter, lay face down in the dirt, her homespun dress streaked with blood. Obi led Thomas behind a fallen log. "I feel as if I just died and went to hell," Thomas whispered.

"We wait here till dark, then we go to the river," Obi told him. They waited, listening to the screams and gunfire, until night fell. Then Obi helped Thomas to his feet and practically carried him down the hill.

The hillside had turned into a steep graveyard. Obi couldn't tell whether a dark form was a body or a log. When they reached the riverbank, Obi eased himself and Thomas among the reeds. He prayed that the gunboat would be there in the morning and find them before the Confederate soldiers did.

Forgetting to play dead, Obi jumped when someone touched his arm. It was daylight and, in spite of the horror, birds sang. Looking up, he saw two Union sailors.

"You okay, soldier? Can you walk?" one of them asked.

Obi nodded and stood up. His legs felt weak and wobbly.

"Thomas still alive?" Obi whispered, afraid of the answer.

"Your friend here?" he asked, leaning over Thomas's still

body. He turned to the other sailor. "If he's alive, we'll put both of them on the gunboat. Otherwise, leave this one for the burial detail."

Obi's head swam and he started to sink back down on the ground.

"Come on now, feller," the sailor said, grabbing Obi by his waist. "We're going to take you to the hospital at Mound City."

Obi sat on the edge of a small cot in the Mound City Hospital. He wore an old army shirt that the hospital had given him. Thomas lay on the cot, his wide eyes open and without their feverish glare. "A nurse tells me only about one hundred of us escaped," Thomas said. "The Rebels tried to kill every living thing." He grimaced as he tried to sit up. Obi helped him.

"The surgeon said I was lucky. The ball hit a joint and didn't shatter my bone. Otherwise he might have had to cut off my leg. You saved my life, Obi."

"Shoot," Obi smiled, "you ain't finish teachin' me to read an' write. Where I get a next teacher from if somethin' happen to you?"

Thomas grinned. "Why don't you come north with me when our time is up?" he asked.

"Can't do that," Obi said.

"Want to search for your mother?"

"No. I know I had a ma, an' I know she love me. Most of us just know they was borned is all." Obi stared for a moment at a man in the bed next to Thomas. He'd lost an arm and was moaning in his sleep. "I see all the death an' fightin'. Life get took away fast as you blink the eye. Lorena the past."

"Come with me, then. My mother will treat you like her own son."

"Have to find Easter an' Jason. Bring them with me if I do come."

He checked for his pouch. "Keep forgettin' I lose my

money an' them papers with the name that ain't mine."

"You can get new papers," Thomas said. He stared at the ceiling. "Got an idea, Obi. This time, tell them the name *you* want."

"Been thinkin' 'bout that. I tell them to change whatever paper they have to the name Buka. Buka say his name mean 'firstborn.' "

"Buka," Thomas repeated. "Guess you spell that *B-o-o-k-e-r*. I'll get a pen and paper from the nurse and write it for you," he said. "Then you tell them when you get your new papers that you're changing your name from Jennings to Booker. Obidiah Booker."

Obi smiled handsomely. "That suit me fine, Thomas. Obidiah Booker."

DATE DUE

Is Harry really as horrible as everyone thinks he is?

After lunch when we were working on math, Harry walked back to check the tank. Then he shouted, "The black molly is floating on the water. She's DEAD!"

Everyone rushed back to the tank.

Miss Mackle opened the cover of the tank and took out the net. She scooped up the dead fish. Then she put her finger in the water. "Why, the water is hot! Someone has been fooling with the temperature knob."

Everyone looked at the thermometer. The mercury was way above the green zone. "Who would do such a horrible thing?" Miss Mackle exclaimed.

Everyone looked at Harry.

PUFFIN BOOKS ABOUT ROOM 2B

HORRIBLE HARRY AND THE ANT INVASION

BY SUZY KLINE

Pictures by Frank Remkiewicz

Puffin Books

PUFFIN BOOKS
Published by the Penguin Group
Penguin Putnam Inc., 375 Hudson Street, New York, New York 10014, U.S.A.
Penguin Books Ltd, 27 Wrights Lane, London W8 5TZ, England
Penguin Books Australia Ltd, Ringwood, Victoria, Australia
Penguin Books Canada Ltd, 10 Alcorn Avenue, Toronto, Ontario, Canada M4V 3B2
Penguin Books (N.Z.) Ltd, 182-190 Wairau Road, Auckland 10, New Zealand

Penguin Books Ltd, Registered Offices: Harmondsworth, Middlesex, England

First published in the United States by Viking Penguin,
a division of Penguin Books USA Inc., 1989
Published in Puffin Books, 1991
Reissued 1998

1 3 5 7 9 10 8 6 4 2

THE LIBRARY OF CONGRESS HAS CATALOGED THE PREVIOUS PUFFIN BOOKS EDITION
UNDER CATALOG CARD NUMBER: 91-53152
This edition ISBN 0-14-130082-5

Printed in the United States of America

RL: 2.5

For my class who launched the original
ant invasion at Southwest School:

Vicki Aiken   Elena Gelzinis
Shannon Barriere   Michael George
Justin Carile   Jimmy Grace
Jennifer Condon   Dean Guenther
Gregory Dahlmann   Shawn Hickey
Dawn DuCotey   Kim Milanese
Andrea Friday   Nathaniel Periera
Ricky Gaudette   Justin St. Pierre
Ryan Garofano   Timothy Tribou

Contents

Horrible Harry
and the Ant
Invasion

When Harry and I walked into Room 2B, we couldn't believe our eyes.

"Look at that!" I said.

"Wow! What is it, Doug?" Harry asked me.

"It's an ant city."

"Ants . . ." Harry grinned. Then he rubbed his hands together.

Harry loves anything that crawls,

slithers, or slides. He loves slimy things, hairy things, and creepy things.

Harry loves anything horrible.

"The ants haven't arrived yet," Miss Mackle said. "But they should come any day now in the mail."

"The mail?" Sidney made a face. "Eeyew. There's going to be ants in Miss Mackle's mailbox."

Harry flashed his white teeth, "Neato . . ." he said. "Are we going to have an ant monitor?"

Miss Mackle looked at the list of jobs on the Monitor Chart. "We're going to need one. Would you be interested, Harry?"

Harry smiled so wide his silver fillings showed in the back.

Miss Mackle printed Harry's name next to Ant Monitor.

One week later when the class was

MONITOR CHART

MESSENGER	Ida
PAPER	Sydney
PLANTS	Doug
SWEEPER	Mary
FISH	Song Lee
ANTS	Harry

lined up in the hall by the office, Miss Mackle checked her mailbox. She found a small manila envelope in it.

When she opened it up, she pulled out a plastic vial. There were a lot of black, hairy things moving around in it.

"THE ANTS!" the class shouted.

The school secretary, Mrs. Foxworth, poked her head around the corner. "Ants . . . ?" she replied.

"We're going to observe their behavior," Miss Mackle said.

Mrs. Foxworth tried to smile, but she was shaking so much the pencil that was sitting on her ear dropped to the floor.

Harry picked it up and handed it to her. "Are you afraid of ants?"

Mrs. Foxworth ran back to her typewriter.

Harry grinned. "She's afraid of ants."

"Well," Miss Mackle said, "the direc-

6

tions on this small package say to put the vial in a refrigerator for ten minutes so the ants will go to sleep. It's easier to put sleeping ants in the ant city."

Harry stepped forward. "I'm the ant monitor. I'll take it to the teachers' refrigerator for you."

Miss Mackle raised her eyebrows.

"Can I pick an assistant?" Harry asked.

Miss Mackle nodded as she looked at the waving hands.

"I pick . . . Doug," Harry said.

I beamed.

Miss Mackle looked relieved.

We walked down the hall to the teachers' room with the vial of ants.

When we opened the refrigerator, we looked for a place to set the vial.

"Gee," I said, "there's so much diet soda in here, it's hard to find room."

Harry finally set the vial on top of a container of banana yogurt.

Then we walked back down the hall.

Mrs. Foxworth was coming toward us. "Hello, boys," she said in a cheery voice.

"Taking your morning break?" Harry asked.

Mrs. Foxworth nodded. "Thought I would have a little banana yogurt."

Harry and I stopped. We looked at each other.

Mrs. Foxworth closed the teachers' room door.

Then we heard it. A shrill scream!

Harry and I walked back to Room 2B laughing.

Ten minutes later Miss Mackle brought the vial of ants back to the classroom.

Everyone gathered around the science table. "I think I should do this, boys and girls," Miss Mackle said. "Some ants bite. I don't want *any* of you to touch one. Is that clear?"

Everyone nodded their heads.

Miss Mackle took the roof off an ant house. Then she took the cap off the vial. We all watched her pour the ants into the small opening.

"Their bodies look like raisins," Ida said.

"That's the way they sleep, Ida, all rolled up," Miss Mackle replied.

"Eeyew," Sidney groaned. "They're gross."

The teacher looked at Sidney. "We are scientists. We are observing ant behavior. Someday, someone in Room 2B may be a great scientist and make great discoveries in a lab."

Harry and I pointed at each other. We

were planning to be great scientists. Someday.

Just as Miss Mackle finished pouring the sleeping ants into the hole, the ants at the bottom of the vial started to wake up.

"Goodness!" Miss Mackle exclaimed.

Sidney screamed when three ants crawled out of the vial onto the science table.

Miss Mackle stood up. "No one move or touch anything. I will get the ants."

"One is on the floor!" Mary called.

Miss Mackle crawled after it. She put a pencil in front of the runaway ant. It crawled up the eraser. Miss Mackle popped the ant into the opening of the ant house, then put the roof back on.

"Two ants are missing," she said. Her hair was in her eyes and one of her high heels was off.

"THEY'RE GOING TO GET US!" Sidney shouted.

"Sidney," Miss Mackle said with her teeth clenched, "we *must* remain calm."

Harry stood in front of the teacher. "As your ant monitor, I will find the missing ants." And then he gave her a salute.

"Just *don't* touch the ants!" Miss Mackle insisted.

Harry took out his lunch box. He unwrapped his sandwich and scraped some peanut butter onto his finger.

Then he put his finger under the science table and waited.

Miss Mackle put her shoe back on, and pushed her hair out of her face. "I think everyone should return to their desks now."

"I found them!" Harry shouted from under the table.

Everyone bent down and looked.

Including Miss Mackle.

There were the two runaway ants on
Harry's finger.

Miss Mackle grabbed her pencil and
quickly scraped them off and then
dropped them into the opening of the
ant city.

Harry flashed a big smile. "I told you
I'd find them."

Miss Mackle frowned. "I told you *not*

to touch the ants. Look at your finger."

Everyone did. There were two red marks.

"He got bit!" Mary exclaimed.

"I think you should go to the nurse," Miss Mackle said. "And when you come back you'll see another name on the Monitor Chart next to Ant Monitor."

Harry put his head down as he walked to the nurse's office.

The next morning, Harry was really quiet. He didn't join our conversation about ants at the science table.

"They bury their own dead," I said.

"They bury their own food," Mary said.

"Eeyew," Sidney replied. "Look, those ants are kissing!"

Miss Mackle walked over to our table. "Ants pass food by kissing. Some-

 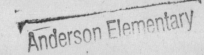

times they send messages that way."

Sidney fell off his chair and rolled over on the floor laughing.

"You may return to your seat, Sidney. Ida is about to feed the ants, and I want only serious scientists to watch."

Sidney frowned as he walked back to his chair.

Harry frowned as he watched Ida doing *his* job.

Ida filled an eye dropper from a bowl

of sugar water. Then, when the teacher removed the roof, Ida squeezed the eye dropper three times into the ant house.

"I'll get it back," Harry whispered to me.

"Get what back?"

"My *ant monitor job*."

I looked at Harry. I could tell he was making plans.

"How?"

"All I have to do is get on the teacher's good side. Then I can ask her for another chance."

Just then Harry tipped back on his chair and his baseball cards came tumbling out of his pocket.

Miss Mackle put her hands on her hips. "Harry, put those things away. Baseball is a distraction in the classroom."

Harry got down on his knees and

picked up his baseball cards.

"I don't want any more antics from you today, Harry," Miss Mackle said.

"*Antics*?" Harry repeated. "That's an *ant* word."

Miss Mackle smiled. "Yes, it is. We have lots of *ant* words in our language. Maybe we should think of some."

Harry clapped his hands.

Mmmmmm, I thought. Harry might just pull it off.

"I'll start," Miss Mackle said. "*Anti*freeze; I had to put some in my car this morning."

"*Antarctica* and *Atlantic*," Mary said, looking at the globe.

"Good, any others?" the teacher asked.

"*Anti*pasto," Mr. Cardini, the principal, said as he showed up at the door.

Everyone laughed.

"My mother makes the best antipasto in the world—salami, cheese, black olives, mmm. . . . Just stopped in to visit the ants," he said, sitting down at the science table.

Miss Mackle continued the lesson.

"Eleph*ant* and p*ant*her," I said, thinking about animals in the zoo.

Harry held up *Jack and the Beanstalk*. "Giant!"

Miss Mackle wrote the new words on the board.

"Fancy," Ida said.

"Nice try, but that doesn't have a *t* in it," Miss Mackle said.

"Ranch?" Sidney asked.

"That is a *c-h* word."

Our class seemed to be stuck.

Then Mr. Cardini saw two ants kissing and he stood up. "I've got one—ro-m*ant*ic!"

Everyone groaned as he waltzed out of the room.

"*I've* got the best ant word," Harry said. Then he pointed to the December calendar. "S*ant*a!"

Everyone cheered and clapped.

Then Harry stood up like he had the biggest idea in the world. "Why don't we draw pictures of ants carrying these words? We could make them go up the stairway and invade the second floor!"

Invasions, I thought. Harry loved them.

Miss Mackle looked at the long list of *ant* words on the board.

"Let's do it!" she said.

Everyone took out their crayons and scissors as the teacher passed out brown paper.

"I'm making a black ant to carry my word, p*ant*her," I said.

"I'm making a HUGE ant to carry my word, gi*ant*," Harry said.

"I'm making a big red heart next to my ant," Mary replied.

Everyone knew what ant word Mary was doing. Rom*ant*ic.

When all the ants were drawn and cut, and the words were neatly printed above, the class lined up in the hall.

Miss Mackle walked us to the stairwell. "Let's hope we have enough to make it to the top!"

"We will!" Harry called out. Then he whispered to me. "We have to. She'll be in such a good mood, she'll give me another chance to be Ant Monitor.

We started taping the ants at the bottom of the wall near the stairs and made a trail going up and down and around the stairway.

When we got to the top, we were one word short.

Everyone sat down on the stairs.

"I knew we couldn't do it," Sidney complained.

"Well," Miss Mackle replied, "maybe tomorrow."

Harry made a face. Then he reached in his back pocket and pulled out three baseball cards. "The Yankees! They won the penn*ant* this year."

"AN *ANT* WORD!" everyone shouted.

Miss Mackle clapped her hands. "Bravo, Harry! You can make the word today and put it up. We reached the second floor thanks to . . ."—and she looked at Harry's baseball cards— "some distractions!"

Harry beamed at his teacher. "If I promise to follow your directions in science, will you give me another chance to be Ant Monitor?"

Miss Mackle put her hand on Harry's shoulder and smiled. "All right, Harry. I don't see why you *can't*."

Harry was horribly happy.

Horrible Harry and the Square Dance

Miss Mackle stood in front of the room. "This Friday we are going to have a square dance."

All the boys groaned.

Except Harry.

I knew what Harry was thinking. He wanted to dance with Song Lee.

Harry has had a crush on Song Lee since the day that she brought in a potato beetle for show-and-tell.

She didn't say anything but she passed a box around with a small striped bug in it.

Harry looked at the bug, then at Song Lee.

It was true love.

Friday afternoon, Miss Mackle led our class down to the gym. She had a record under her arm. It was called "Let's Square Dance."

"Now," she said. "I want the boys to line up behind Sidney, and the girls to line up behind Mary."

"I don't want to dance with her," Sidney said, looking at Mary across from him.

Miss Mackle put the record down and then she looked at Sidney. She had her hands on her hips.

"Sidney, one of the reasons I have dancing is that we need to learn manners."

Sidney put his head down.

"We must say thank you to everyone we dance with. Being polite is very important."

After a moment of silence, Miss Mackle added. "ANYBODY who doesn't agree can dance with the teacher after school—when we'll go over these rules."

Sidney turned green.

All the girls giggled.

All the boys groaned. I did, too. Dancing with the teacher would be deadly.

Miss Mackle showed the girls how to curtsy.

Then she showed the boys how to bow.

Everyone practiced.

I made a face. I hate to dance. When I looked across the floor, I looked at my partner.

It was Song Lee.

Harry gave me a jab in the side. "Move over," he said. "I'm dancing with her."

I didn't mind at all. There were more boys than girls, and no one was standing next to Song Lee.

"You have Miss X," Miss Mackle said to me.

I beamed. Dancing with no one wasn't bad at all.

Miss Mackle then showed us how to do the Virginia reel.

Harry walked over and took Song Lee's hands. He wanted to get ready early.

"Not yet," Miss Mackle said. "I haven't even turned the music on."

Everyone laughed.

Harry held up his fist.

When the music finally did go on, the boys walked across the floor and bowed.

The girls walked across the floor and curtsied.

"Now let's do the Virginia reel!" Miss Mackle called.

Sidney walked over and took Mary's hands. His eyes were closed.

They sashayed down the center.

And then they joined their lines.

"You didn't stop and twirl her under your arm," Miss Mackle complained.

Harry was next.

He walked over and took Song Lee's hands and then they sashayed down the center. He stopped, put up his arm, and Song Lee twirled around and then curtsied.

Harry bowed so low his curly hair touched his knees.

"Bravo!" Miss Mackle said.

Harry flashed his white teeth.

Song Lee looked down at her black shoes.

When I came down with Miss X, everyone laughed.

The next time we went through the line we had new partners. I had Ida. Sidney had Song Lee.

When Sidney went over to take Song Lee's hands, he had his eyes closed again. He didn't want to dance with a girl.

Instead of looking where he was going, he walked right into her, and they bumped heads.

Song Lee put her hand on her forehead. There was a big bump and a red mark on her forehead. She was trying not to cry but everyone could see the tears on her cheek.

Harry raised a fist at Sidney.

Miss Mackle sent Song Lee to the nurse. Then she said, "We will have one more dance. Sidney, you must be more careful."

"He should keep his eyes open," I said.

Miss Mackle walked over to Sidney. "Were you dancing with your eyes closed?"

Sidney shook his head. "Nope. They were wide open all the time, like this."

The class stared at Sidney's eyes. They looked like giant white gumballs. Then he made them revolve around and around.

Miss Mackle turned to put the needle on the record.

Harry raised two fists. I knew what he was thinking. Double revenge.

When we returned to the classroom, Song Lee was sitting in her chair with

an ice bottle held against her forehead.

Just before the three-o'clock bell
rang, Harry offered to take the bottle
back to the nurse for her.

Song Lee thanked him and then went
out of the classroom to get her coat.

As the rest of the class lined up to go
home, Harry said, "Hey, Sidney. Meet
me at the corner. I have a little present
for you."

"You do?" Sidney said.

Harry flashed his white teeth. "I do."

Sidney waited for Harry at the corner. "What are you giving me a present for?" he asked when he saw Harry.

"For that trick you did in dancing today."

"Trick?" Sidney couldn't remember.

"You bumped into Song Lee because your eyes were shut."

"Yeah! She even had to go to the nurse with the alligator purse!" Sidney said, bursting into laughter. "So where's my present?"

"Right here," Harry said, flipping the ice bottle and pouring it down Sidney's back.

"Yeooooooow! *That's* COLD!" Sidney screamed as he ran up the street waving his hands in the air. "I'll get even with you for this. Just wait!"

I looked at Harry. "Where did you get that bottle of ice water?"

"From Song Lee. I told her I would return the bottle to the nurse."

And then Harry flashed his white teeth. "I didn't say I would return the melted ice inside."

I cracked up.

"Ol' Sidney had it coming," Harry mumbled.

I waited at the school steps while Harry returned the empty bottle to the nurse.

Sometimes when Harry tells you he's going to do something, he leaves the horrible part out.

Horrible Harry
and
the Deadly Fish
Tank

We have a fish tank in Room 2B. Last time Harry and I counted there were twenty-five fish swimming around in it.

Twenty guppies.

Four neon fish.

And one black molly.

Then there was horrible Monday. This is how it happened.

Sidney came to school mad. He was

mad about Harry putting ice water down his back on Friday.

Even his hair looked angry. It stood on end. Sidney probably didn't bother combing it.

Miss Mackle looked at the Monitor Chart. "Boys and girls, I will announce the week's new monitors. Sidney is Messenger, Doug is Paper Monitor, Ida is Ant Monitor, Mary is Plant Monitor, Song Lee is Sweeper, and . . ." When she finally got to Harry, she said, "Harry is Fish Monitor."

Harry immediately got up and went back to feed the fish. He turned on the light in the tank and took roll. Carefully he recorded the number in the Fish Roll Book.

Then he checked the temperature. It was in the green part of the thermometer—in the 70–80 degree range.

At lunchtime, Harry fed the fish and then lined up behind me in the cafeteria. "I have my favorite dessert, Doug, he said. "Two pieces of Mom's homemade fudge. I'm saving it for us on the way home from school."

I drooled. I know how good Harry's mother's fudge was. Chocolatey, nutty, and mmmmmmmm good.

After lunch when we were working on math, Harry walked back to check the tank. The he shouted, "The black molly is floating on the water. She's DEAD!"

Everyone rushed back to the tank.

Miss Mackle opened the cover of the tank and took out the net. She scooped up the dead fish. Then she put her finger in the water. "Why, the water is hot! Someone has been fooling with the temperature knob."

Everyone looked at the thermometer. The mercury was way above the green zone. "Who would do such a horrible thing?" Miss Mackle exclaimed.

Everyone looked at Harry.

I did too. Harry loves to do horrible things.

Miss Mackle waited for someone to speak.

Sidney spoke first. "Harry is the fish monitor. He did it!"

"Do you know anything about this?" Miss Mackle asked Harry.

Harry shook his head.

Miss Mackle said we wouldn't be doing "little theater" that afternoon. She didn't feel like doing anything fun. She was too disappointed.

We just worked at our seats the rest of the afternoon.

It was a long day.

When Harry lined up at three o'clock, no one wanted to stand next to him.

Except me.

"Do you think I did it?" Harry asked as we walked home.

I didn't say anything. I wasn't sure.

"Doug," Harry said. "I wouldn't do anything *that* horrible. I plan on being a great scientist someday. With you, remember? I would never take the life of a single living thing. Not a beetle, or an ant, or a single blade of grass."

I knew Harry never mowed the lawn. He told his mother he couldn't kill the grass.

We walked home without talking. We didn't even eat Harry's homemade fudge. We just didn't feel like it. The next morning, Harry made a poster and put it up by the fish tank. It was a picture of a tombstone and a graveyard. It said GOD BLESS R BLAK MOLLY.

Then in the top part was a bunch of fish with yellow wings and halos flying around.

"What's that up there?" I asked.

"Fish heaven," Harry replied.

Miss Mackle started the morning as usual with a conversation.

"Boys and girls, we need to talk about our fish. We are responsible for them. Somehow, we made an error."

Sidney raised his hand. "Harry is the

fish monitor. He likes to do horrible things. Harry did it. He should stay after school." Then he sat back in his chair and smiled.

I looked at Sidney. Then it dawned on me. Revenge. That's what Sidney wanted! He wanted to get even because Harry had put ice water down his back.

Harry raised his fist at Sidney. "I wouldn't cook a fish like that."

"Prove it!" Sidney replied.

"Harry," Miss Mackle said, "do you know anything about how the black molly died?"

Harry shook his head.

Everyone made a face. No one believed Harry but me.

"Did anyone see someone at the fish tank just before the lunch bell? I asked.

Song Lee had her hand in the air for the *first* time.

"Yes, Song Lee," Miss Mackle said. "Did you see someone?"

Softly, Song Lee spoke, "I see Sidney by the tank just before bell ring. He reach behind where knob is."

Sidney sank down in his chair.

Miss Mackle glared at him.

Sidney looked at the teacher, then the class. His face turned red. "I didn't

mean to kill the fish. I just . . . just . . ."

"Just what?" Miss Mackle asked.

". . . wanted to get"—Sidney's voice got softer and softer—"Harry in trouble."

"We'll talk about it after school," Miss Mackle said firmly.

Harry looked over at Song Lee.
And beamed.

Harry really isn't *that* horrible. On a scale of 1–10, he probably is a 7 for horribleness.

Then I noticed Harry get up and get his lunch box. He took something out of it and gave it to Song Lee.

It was the two pieces of homemade fudge!

Forget that 7. Anyone who gives *my* fudge away to a *girl* is a 10!

Horrible Harry and the Class Picture

Tuesday everyone came to school looking very neat. It was picture day for Room 2B.

"How nice everyone looks!" Miss Mackle exclaimed.

We looked at the teacher's hairdo. It was really curly. And it looked red.

"Did you dye your hair?" Mary asked the teacher.

Miss Mackle's face turned red. "No, I just"—her voice got softer—"just used a red rinse."

"You look pretty," Harry said. And then he flashed his white teeth.

"Thank you, Harry, you look quite nice in your suit and tie."

"My mother made me wear it. She's ordering pictures for all my relatives for Christmas."

"Will we get free combs this year?" Sidney blurted out.

"Let's hope so," Mary said. "You need one."

Everyone looked at Sidney. His hair stuck out all over his head.

Miss Mackle took out her red attendance book. "Let's see, everyone is here today except . . . Song Lee?"

We looked around. She wasn't at her desk or next to the fish tank or sharpening a pencil.

Harry frowned. "Do you think she's sick?"

"I hope not," Miss Mackle said. "It would be so nice to have everyone present for the picture."

Just then, Song Lee appeared at the door.

Harry's eyebrows shot up.

Miss Mackle went to meet her. "Why, Song Lee, you look beautiful."

Song Lee looked down at the floor. Her hair was in a bun. Two white flowers were pinned on either side of her hair.

She was wearing a long dress and a flowered sash. When Song Lee looked up she said, "Mother want to send picture to Korea for my relatives."

Miss Mackle smiled. "They will be very pleased."

Just then Mrs. Foxworth appeared at the door. "The photographer is ready for Room 2B in the gym now."

As we walked down the hall, I said to Harry, "We probably won't get to stand next to each other. I'm four inches taller than you."

"I know," Harry replied. "I'll probably be next to the king of hairdos."

I knew who Harry meant.

Sidney.

"Maybe you'll get lucky," I said.

"What do you mean?" Harry asked.

"You might be next to Song Lee."

Harry looked at me and grinned.

"You might be next to the teacher," Harry said.

I frowned.

When we got in the gym, a mother

passed out orange combs. Another mother went up to each student and helped to comb their hair. When she got to Sidney, she couldn't get his snarls out.

Then the comb broke.

"Okay, kiddies!" the photographer said. "Line up over here."

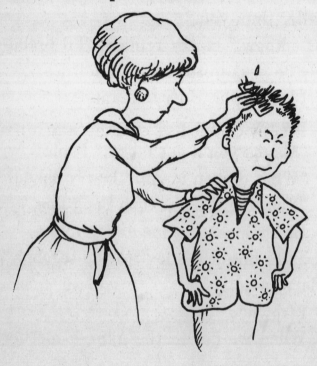

When he saw Harry in his suit and Song Lee in her outfit, he said, "Ooh la la! Look who's getting married today!"

Everyone laughed and giggled.

Harry held up a fist. "I'm going to be a great scientist when I grow up. I'm not getting married."

Song Lee kept looking at her sash.

"Well, you two make a great couple. You can hold the sign that says, MISS MACKLE'S SECOND GRADE CLASS."

Sidney cackled so loud, he was hurting my eardrums.

"And you two gorgeous redheads can stand together!" the photographer said.

Then he moved Sidney and the teacher together.

Everyone laughed again. Except Sidney.

"Hey, good-looking," the photographer said to me, "you get to stand between two lovely ladies."

I made a face and stood between Ida and Mary.

"Okay, kiddies," the photographer said. "Say hamburger with pickles and cheese!"

The photographer flashed his camera.

"Now say liver and onions!"

The photographer flashed his camera again.

I was hoping the pictures would be over really soon. I was surrounded by girls.

"Say spaghetti and meatballs!"

The photographer flashed his camera one last time.

MISS MACKLE'S
SECOND
GRADE CLASS

"I hope I didn't close my eyes," Miss Mackle said.

Harry put the sign down on the floor. Then he lined up by the ramp.

I could tell Harry was miffed about something. He took off his tie and stuffed it in his pocket.

When I stood next to him, he whispered. "I don't like that guy."

"You mean the photographer?"

Harry nodded.

"Yeah," I said. "I think he should open a restaurant and sell liver and onions, spaghetti and meatballs, and hamburgers with pickles."

Harry looked at me and then at the photographer. "That guy was acting so dumb I wouldn't buy a picture *or* a pickle from him."

Harry always tells the horrible truth.

ABOUT THE AUTHOR

Suzy Kline graduated from the University of California at Berkeley and received her elementary school teacher's credential from California State University at Hayward. She has been teaching for sixteen years and is the author of the popular Herbie Jones series (available in Puffin). Kline was selected Teacher of the Year in 1986 by the Torrington School District in Connecticut and in 1988 by the Probus Club of Torrington.